Taking Your Place In Christ

Mark Hankins

Taking Your Place
In Christ

Mark Hankins

Mark Hankins Ministries
Alexandria, Louisiana

Taking Your Place In Christ

ISBN 978-1-889981-16-1
Copyright (c) 1996 by Mark Hankins Ministries
Mark Hankins Ministries
P. O. Box 12863
Alexandria, LA 71315

Published by MHM Publications

3rd Edition 2007, Revised, First Printing 20,000 copies in print.
More than 20,000 copies of the 2nd Edition in print.
More than 40,000 copies of the 1st Edition in print.

CONTENTS

1

A MAN IN CHRIST

Therefore if any man be in Christ, he is a new creature: old things are passed away; behold all things are become new.

2 Corinthians 5:17

Jesus did not go through the agony of the crucifixion, death, burial, and resurrection just to help us a little bit. What happened from the cross to the throne in those three days changed everything. Radical changes happened in Christ. These are not minor events listed in history with such things as the Wright Brothers with the invention of the airplane or Lewis and Clark with the great expedition. This is the main event of all time and eternity.

What Jesus did changed all of heaven and earth — seen and unseen. He is the "firstborn from the dead." He is the first

1

man to enter death's domain and conquer it. Jesus is Lord! When He arose from the dead, He took His blood into the heavenly holy place as a man to purchase our eternal freedom. Jesus took us with Him. We can follow the blood covenant trail right into the very presence of God. We have the same access, privilege, and confidence as Jesus. The same power that is in these events is in the Gospel. As we feed on the Word, we partake of the same power that happened two thousand years ago in these world-changing events. A man in Christ is a world-changing man.

The world is constantly fantasizing about Superman, Wonder Woman, Batman, Hercules, the Bionic Woman, the Six Million Dollar Man, Jedi Knights, and the Incredible Hulk. Each of these individuals is an amazing specimen among us. Many stories have been told and movies made about these unusual creatures. However, God has produced the real thing — the most amazing specimen of all. He has created a man in Christ. This is no man-made fantasy. God has made a new creature that is a sign and a wonder in this world.

A MAN IN CHRIST IS A NEW CREATURE

The Greek word translated "new" means unheard of before. It means new in quality or kind. A man in Christ is a new kind of man, a new breed or species that never existed before. You are not just a new person individually, but a new kind of person. You are not just a forgiven sinner, you are a new creation with a new kind of life. A man in Christ is a partaker of the life and nature of God.

> *And this is the record, that God hath given to us eternal life, and this life is in his Son. He that hath the Son hath life; and he that hath not the Son of God hath not life. These things have I written unto you that believe on the name of the Son of God; that you may know that you have eternal life, and that you may believe on the name of the Son of God.*
>
> *1 John 5:11-13*

This life which flows from God into man is something totally different from anything experienced on the natural plane. It is different not only in degree but also in kind. It is supernatural life. It makes man a new creation. It is not the intensification of powers already possessed, but the sudden emergence of an entirely new and original element. When a man comes to be in Christ he begins to live in the post-resurrection life of Christ. The life he now lives bears the quality of eternity.

A Man In Christ, James Stewart

THE GOD-KIND OF LIFE

I like the phrase "a sudden emergence of an entirely new and original element." We become partakers of the life of God—suddenly! Through simple faith in Jesus Christ, the miracle of the new birth takes place in the spirit of the believer. Eternal life is a spiritual substance from heaven that is imparted in the spirit of a man.

> *Eternal life is not simply life that goes on forever. It is true that the New Testament never forgets that God has promised men resurrection from the dead, but the essential of eternal life is not duration, it is quality. Eternal life is the injection into the realm of time of something of the realm of eternity. It is the coming into human life of something of the life of God.*
>
> *William Barclay*

LIFE AS GOD HAS IT

God has given us a new quality of life in Christ. He has given us His own life — the very same life that raised Jesus from the dead (Ephesians 2:4-6). He has given us eternal life. God wants us to know that we have eternal life now. We are not trying to get it or some day in the sweet-by-and-by going to get it. We know we have a present possession; we have eternal life. The gift of God is eternal life (Romans 6:23). What a great gift God has given us in Christ!

The Greek word in the New Testament for *life* or *eternal life* is zoe. This life is the primary purpose Jesus came. Jesus said, "I am come that you might have life, and that you might have it more abundantly," John 10:10. This life is a spiritual substance that flows in heaven from the throne of God; it flows like a river (John 7:37-39). God is overflowing with this life. You and I can have more and more of this life flowing in us. We can have this life in ever-increasing measures as we are filled with the Word of God and the Holy Spirit. We can walk in the light of this life and in the consciousness of what we have in Christ as we learn more and more of the "words of this life" (Acts 5:20).

ETERNAL LIFE: PRESENT ACTUAL POSSESSION

I like *W.E. Vine's* definition of the word "zoe" (eternal life, everlasting life, or life).

> *It is life as a principle...life in the absolute sense, as God has it, that which the Father has in Himself and which He gave to the incarnate Son to have in Himself (John 5:26). It is what the Son*

manifested in the world (1 John 1:1,2). From this life man has become alienated through the fall and of this life men become partakers through faith in the Lord Jesus Christ, who becomes its author to all who trust in Him. The life He gives, He maintains. Eternal life is the present actual possession of the believer because of his relationship with Christ, and that it will one day extend its domain to the sphere of the body is assured by the resurrection of Christ.

GOD SEES YOU IN CHRIST

A man in Christ is a man with the life of God. You are not deity, but you are not only human. You have been born of God. God has given you His very own life. You are a new creature — something that never existed before. You are such a new creature in Christ, you will have to let God introduce you to your new self. You are not the same person you used to be. God sees you in Christ, but you must also see yourself in Him. You will never be different until you see yourself differently. The Holy Spirit takes the things of Christ and shows them to us (John 16:13-15). He is able to project the image of Christ from the Word to the screen of our minds, so we can live in the reality of our redemption.

SEEING WHAT GOD SEES

Paul's prayer for believers in Ephesians 1:16-23 is very important for us today. "I pray that you new Christians will understand the mighty position with Christ which your congregations occupy" (verse 16, The Distilled Bible). We have a mighty position with Christ. Few Christians have understood the authority we have as believers. The same mighty power that raised Christ from the dead was released "towards us." We were the target of that power. God was focusing on us. He was looking at us. God saw us there in Christ. He was working on us. We are His workmanship created in Christ Jesus (Ephesians 2:10). What God

> You are such a new creature in Christ, you will have to let God introduce you to your new self.

did in Christ, He did in us. Paul's prayer is our prayer today that we can see and enjoy the life God has given us in Christ. I like to say it this way: If you are not impressed with who you are and what you have in Christ, you have not seen Him lately.

I like what James Stalker says in his book, *The Life of Paul,*

> *Paul's letters contain the thoughts that Jesus carried away from this world unuttered. They are the advanced teachings of our Lord Jesus Christ.*

7

The Epistles are the letters written to the church today. They contain the thoughts that Jesus is thinking now. We must study the epistles to grow up in Christ.

In 2 Corinthians 12:2, the Apostle Paul refers to himself as, "a man in Christ." He could not tell whether he was in the body or out of the body. Paul even ascended into the third heaven. A man in Christ is not just of this world, but he also has access to heaven.

ACT LIKE THE BIBLE IS TRUE

And be renewed in the spirit of your mind; And that you put on the new man, which after God is created in righteousness and true holiness.

Ephesians 4:23,24

You can know that the Bible says these things about you, but they may not seem real to you. We have a part to play. We must put on the new man. We did not make the new man. God did that. We must put on the new man. That is our part. One translation says, "...put on the new person that you are." This new man is created in righteousness and true holiness. God would not make an unrighteous new creature. You have been made the righteousness of God in Christ (2 Corinthians 5:21).

God sees you through the blood of Jesus. He looks at you as though you never did anything wrong. As the old Gospel

8

song says, "There is a fountain filled with blood drawn from Emmanuel's veins, and sinners plunged beneath that flood lose all their guilty stains." The power of the blood of Jesus washes away *all* the guilty stains and we can stand in God's presence confidently. We can face life confidently. We can pray confidently. In Christ we have right standing with God. It is not only right standing with God; it is the identical standing with the Father that Jesus has. Dare to see yourself this way!

Take time to renew your mind every day with the reality of redemption. Dare to act like the Bible is true, and it will become real in your life. Allow God to introduce you to your new self. Daily declare:

> *I am a new creature in Christ Jesus. I have God's very own life and nature in me. The life of God is in me now. I know I have eternal life. The law of the spirit of life in Christ Jesus has made me free from the law of sin and death. In Christ, I am redeemed, blessed, and victorious. I am the righteousness of God in Christ. In Christ I am delivered from the power of darkness and translated into the kingdom of the Son of God. In Christ I have redemption through His blood, even the forgiveness of sins.*

Paul's letters contain the
thoughts that Jesus carried away
from this world
unuttered. They are the
advanced teachings of our
Lord Jesus Christ.
- James Stalker

If anyone has entered into fellowship
with Christ, a new world has at once
opened upon him, an old world has
passed away.
2 Corinthians 5:17, STANLEY

2

ONCE UPON A TIME

Everyone likes a great story that begins with the phrase, "Once upon a time...." The story of Jesus is the greatest story ever told. It is not a fantasy, but a true story that has changed the world for thousands of years. The story of Jesus is told in over a thousand languages to millions of people, young and old, around the world and is still changing lives today! One day as I was studying Hebrews 9 and 10, the word "ONCE" stood out so clearly. I began to see God's plan of redemption in Christ and how the wisdom and power of God very effectively "ONCE" paid the price for our freedom.

> *Neither by the blood of goats and calves, but by his own blood he entered in ONCE into the holy place, having obtained eternal redemption for us.*
>
> *Hebrews 9:12*

> *He went ONCE for all into the [Holy of]*
> *Holies... but His own blood, having found and*
> *secured a complete redemption (an everlasting*
> *release for us).*
>
> > *Amplified*

ONCE! That's all it took! What Jesus did for us in His death, burial, and resurrection, He only had to do ONCE! He shed His blood, ONCE! He paid the price for our freedom, ONCE! He put away and abolished sin, ONCE! He defeated and dethroned Satan, ONCE FOR ALL TIME...ONCE for all mankind...ONCE for the cure of every condition...ONCE for every blessing in Heaven to be ours!

Whenever you face any challenge, remember this story and tell it again: Once Upon a Time! When Satan comes against you, just bring up this story and say, "Once upon a time..." and he will leave. Now, we as believers can take the Word of God and tell the devil a bedtime story. Say, "Devil, ONCE upon a time Jesus defeated you for all eternity." Speak the Word of God with boldness and rock the devil to sleep!

> *What Jesus did for us in His death, burial, and resurrection, He only had to do ONCE!*

> *So Christ was ONCE offered to bear the sins of*
> *many; and unto them that look for him shall he*

appear the second time without sin unto salvation.

> *Hebrews 9:28*

By the which will we are sanctified through the offering of the body of Jesus Christ ONCE for all.

> *Hebrews 10:10*

For by ONE offering he hath perfected for ever them that are sanctified.

> *Hebrews 10:14*

By looking at these scriptures we see that Jesus cancelled and abolished sin ONCE for all time and for all men. The Holy Spirit continues to emphasize the word "ONCE." We must know this story well. It is the story of Christmas, Easter, Pentecost, Heaven, and Earth. This story is well known by angels and demons. The story of the blood of Jesus is an established fact throughout eternity.

A NEW DAY OF BOLDNESS

The other word that stood out to me in Hebrews was the word *boldness*. The blood of Jesus has given us great boldness and confidence.

Having therefore, brethren, BOLDNESS to enter into the holiest by the blood of Jesus.

Hebrews 10:19

Let us therefore come BOLDLY unto the throne of grace....

Hebrews 4:16

...that we may BOLDLY say, The Lord is my helper....

Hebrews 13:6

Some other translations of Hebrews 10:19 translate boldness as *freedom of speech* or *outspoken*. The blood of Jesus has given us great boldness and confidence. As believers, we need to exercise our freedom of speech and be outspoken about the blood of Jesus and who we are in Christ. Instead of being a victim of our experiences, our experiences are a victim of us.

Notes:

15

If you are not impressed

with who you are

In Christ,

you have not seen him lately.

Therefore, if anyone is in union with Christ,

he is a new being! His old life has passed

away; a new life has begun!

2 Corinthians 5:17, 20th C.R.

3

C H A P T E R T H R E E :

ENGRAFTED INTO CHRIST

The two words "In Christ" are the most important words used by the Apostle Paul in the New Testament. A.J. Gordon said it this way, "These two words 'In Christ' give us profound insight into the Divine method of salvation. These two words open to us mysteries and secrets that were hidden for ages and generations." These words are the key to opening the secrets of the Gospel. We have been *In Christed.* There are over 130 scriptures that use the phrase *In Christ, In Him,* and *In Whom.* What do these phrases mean?

> *Therefore if any person is [ENGRAFTED] in Christ (the Messiah) he is a new creation (a new creature altogether); the old [previous moral and spiritual condition] has passed away. Behold the fresh and new has come!*
>
> *2 Corinthians 5:17, Amplified*

17

I live in an area where there are a lot of plant nurseries. These nurseries have millions and millions of plants that are shipped all over the United States. One thing I have learned from the nurseries is the engrafting process.

Graft – to insert (a shoot from one plant) into another living plant so that the two grow together as a single plant.

The stock of the plant must be cut with the same identical wound as the branch in order for the two to grow together. Then, you must put that branch inside of the open wound of the plant and wrap them together and they will become one.

We have been engrafted into Christ. He is the vine and we are the branches. On the cross, Jesus was wounded with our identical condition and we were placed In Him. There is no *grafting* without wounding.

Surely he hath borne our griefs, and carried our sorrows: yet we did esteem him stricken, smitten of God, and afflicted. But he was WOUNDED for our transgressions, he was bruised for our iniquities: the chastisement of

our peace was upon him; and with his stripes
we are healed.

Isaiah 53:4-5

Jesus took our guilt, shame, sin, death, and curse so that we could be free. We were engrafted into His death that we might be one with His resurrection and victory. He was made to be sin for us that we might be made the righteousness of God In Him (2 Corinthians 5:21).

We are new creatures In Christ and God would not make an unrighteous new creature. We have the same righteousness as Jesus Christ Himself. He took our shame that we may live without guilt. We can now face life confident that we are qualified for God's best blessings.

For the scripture saith, Whosoever believeth on
him shall not be ashamed.

Romans 10:11

In the body of his flesh through death, to
present you holy and unblameable and
unreproveable in his sight.

Colossians 1:22

SHAME-FREE LIVING

Shame is the issue that drives almost every compulsive, self-defeating behavior known to the human race. Shame is at the root of all addictions. It may be forgotten, hidden, or disguised, but the shame is there, is real, and it drives behavior. Sometimes the shame surfaces first. In other cases, the addiction surfaces first. Whenever we encounter one, we always look for the other. Shame and addiction can always be found together.

The Complete Life Encyclopedia

It is especially interesting that professional psychiatrists recognize the power and influence of shame in shaping people today. It drives human behavior. Many have misdiagnosed their own problems and conditions. This has caused many to try to fix their behavior with more and more doses of shame and guilt. Instead of curing the problem, shame perpetuates the problem.

> We look a lot better In Christ than we do outside of Him.

The cure is at the cross of Jesus Christ. On the cross, God was working in Christ but He was working on us. Jesus took our condition and we were engrafted into Him. Now, God sees us in Christ. We must consistently see ourselves in the light of the death, burial, and resurrection. We look a lot better in Christ than we do outside of Him. He sees us through the blood, through the cross, and through the resurrection. He has raised us up together with Christ and seated us together with Him. We reign in life through the abundance of grace and the gift of righteousness through one man Jesus Christ (Romans 5:17).

RIGHTEOUSNESS: REVELATION AND MOTIVATION

It is important to understand that the Gospel of Christ is a revelation of righteousness (Romans 1:17). Understanding righteousness is fundamental to Christianity. Understanding righteousness also enables us to win the fight of faith. The Apostle Paul's letters help us to understand that righteousness is a free gift. His letters also help us to see ourselves *In Christ*.

Righteousness gives us right standing with God. Righteousness sets us free from a sense of sin, guilt, and shame. Since we are free from the motivating power of shame, we are now under a new motivating power of righteousness. The power of righteousness is the revelation of all true victory. We are no longer haunted by a sense of inadequacy or inferiority. God has given us *first-class* righteousness in Christ!

God sees you In Christ,

but you must see yourself

In Him.

You look a whole lot better

In Christ

than you do outside

of Him.

For if anybody is in union with Christ, he

is the work of a new creation; the old

condition has passed away, a

new condition has come.

2 Corinthians 5:17, WMS

4

FINDING YOUR PLACE IN CHRIST

A traveling man entered a town looking for a certain address. He pulled into the driveway of a home where a little boy was playing in the front yard to ask for directions. He rolled down his window and called to the little boy, "Where am I?" The little boy answered, "Right there you are!"

When you go into a large shopping mall, a map is usually posted identifying the different stores that are available on each level. It still may be difficult, however, to find your way around without a note on the map that says, "You are here." Understanding where you are has everything to do with finding your destiny and direction in life. Many times in life we search for answers and direction. God shows us in His Word a simple, "Right there you are!"

Understanding the new birth and who you are in Christ begins with several "right there you are" and "you are here" scriptures. There are more than 130 scriptures that locate who you are and what you have in Christ.

> *Therefore if any man be in Christ, he is a new creature: old things are passed away; behold, all things are become new.*
>
> *2 Corinthians 5:17*

> *For he hath made him to be sin for us, who knew no sin; that we might be made the righteousness of God in him.*
>
> *2 Corinthians 5:21*

> *For in him dwelleth all the fullness of the Godhead bodily. And ye are complete in him, which is the head of all principality and power.*
>
> *Colossians 2:9,10*

> *Now thanks be unto God, which always causeth us to triumph in Christ, and maketh manifest the savour of his knowledge by us in every place.*
>
> *2 Corinthians 2:14*

Accept the integrity of God's Word and boldly declare, "I am who God says I am. I have what God says I have. I can do what God says I can do." Right there you are — in Christ!

My dad and mom pastored a full gospel church in West Columbia, Texas for more than 50 years. The Christian Center has grown to be the largest church in West Columbia and the largest Full Gospel church in the area.

When my parents first moved to West Columbia, I was only a year old and my older brother, Mike, was four. Mom was sick and mentally tormented for the first two years in West Columbia. Dad not only pastored the church, but also had the pressure of all the family responsibilities. Dad began to have heart trouble. During this same time, while playing outside with Mike, I stuck my thumb into a bicycle chain and cut off my thumb. I don't remember ever having two thumbs! The church was small and struggling, and we were poor. It was a tough time for us.

However, in the middle of this struggle a man gave my dad some books on the authority of the believer, the integrity of God's Word, and who you are in Christ. Dad began to read and study the material and gained a new understanding of God's Word.

> *The entrance of thy words giveth light; it giveth understanding unto the simple.*
>
> *Psalm 119:130*

Dad began to speak the Word to Mom and had her repeat it after him. She began to say, "I am who God says I am. I have what God says I have. I can do what God says I can do!" As my parents saw who they were in Christ and spoke the Word, faith arose in their hearts. They knew that victory belonged to them in every area of their life.

IT'S NOT NECESSARY, UNLESS IT'S NECESSARY

As I grew up in church, there were some *unusual* services. Sometimes while we sang, Mom would begin to praise God rather exuberantly and shout, "Hallelujah! Hallelujah! Hallelujah!" With glory and joy on her countenance, she would shout "Wooooo!" and run around the church! Dad was a little more dignified. After Mom ran, Dad would say, "Now, some of you don't think that is necessary. It's not necessary, unless it's necessary!" While the congregation tried to figure out what Dad had said, Mom and others who had joined her would finish their rejoicing!

When I became a teenager, this was very embarrassing to me. When we were encouraged to bring visitors to church, I would say, "I'm not going to bring my friends to this church...I would never live it down." One day a friend of mine showed up in our church. I certainly hadn't invited him! As soon as I saw him, I went and sat by him and began to pray, "O God, please don't let this be a wild service, and please don't let my mother run." That's a dangerous prayer!

MY MOTHER RUNS

About that time, people began to sense the power of God and started rejoicing. The Holy Spirit fell on the entire place. My friend's eyes got big. I tried to comfort him and tell him everything would be all right. Then my mother began to say, "Hallelujah! Hallelujah! Hallelujah!" I thought, "Oh no, she's revving up her engine." Sure enough, I heard a "Woooooo!" and she started running around the church.

I put my head down, and my friend asked, "Who is that woman?" I said, "I have no idea! We get all kinds of unusual people in here!" I made sure he never came to my house. I was ashamed of the power of God and had little understanding or appreciation of the pit my mother had come out of.

> *He brought me up also out of an horrible pit, and out of the miry clay, and set my feet upon a rock, and established my goings. And he hath put a new song in my mouth, even praise unto our God...*
>
> *Psalm 40:2,3*

I did not understand the magnitude of my mother's deliverance, until I was seventeen and running from God. I had an automobile accident coming home from a party with a backslidden friend that totaled several cars. We walked away without a scratch. My backslidden friend said, "If your mom wasn't praying, we would have been killed." I agreed.

SATAN HATH DESIRED TO HAVE YOU

When I got home, Mom was sitting in a rocking chair. She spoke the words that Jesus spoke to Peter, "...Satan hath desired to have you, that he might sift you as wheat: but I have prayed for thee, that thy faith fail not: and when thou art converted, strengthen thy brethren," Luke 22:31,32.

Although good changes had begun in my life, not long after the automobile accident three friends and I ended up in the county jail. I called Mom from the jail and she said, "Your dad has church tonight (it was a Wednesday night), so just prop your feet up and stay a while!" Dad and four deacons came to jail after church and put up bond for me so I could go home. After that incident, I sold my '55 Chevrolet and that sobered me up for a while!

ARRESTED BY GOD

One Sunday God had a surprise for me. I was sitting on the back row cutting up, and God "arrested" me. An unannounced guest speaker, F.E. Ward, came to church that Sunday. Brother Ward was a big, stocky preacher. You never knew when he was going to show up, and that Sunday I was not prepared for what was about to happen.

Since our church believed in the baptism of the Holy Spirit and the gifts of the Spirit, the supernatural was often in manifestation. Sometimes preachers would call someone out and give them a Word from the Lord. Usually, I knew when they were coming, and I would repent of all my sins in the foyer before I came into the auditorium. I knew the Bible said that if we asked God to forgive us, He would forgive and even forget our transgressions. I thought, "If God forgets it, then He can't tell that preacher, and that preacher can't tell the whole church."

But that Sunday I was sitting on the back row with my backslidden friends when Brother Ward went to the platform and said he felt led to do something. He pointed to the back and said, "I want the pastor's son to come to the front." I was shocked! My friends made a comment, "You're a dead duck now!" As I got up and headed down the aisle, I began to repent under my breath: "O God, forgive me of my sins! Please don't tell that preacher what I've been doing. If You tell him and he tells everybody, my dad will kill me."

All the blood drained from my face, and I was afraid and embarrassed as I stood in front of the whole church. I was only seventeen, but I thought my life had come to an end! I fully expected God to bring out a giant flyswatter and squash me in front of the whole church. I expected a voice from heaven to say, "Let this young man be an example to the rest of you in this church. Put twelve stones on this greasy spot and tell your kids about it!"

Instead, I heard the voice of F.E. Ward say, "Sit down on the altar." As I sat down, he began to speak to me under the inspiration of the Holy Spirit. As he spoke to me about God's plan and purpose for my life, the presence and love of God overwhelmed me, and I began to cry. I surrendered my life to Jesus again, and my heart was changed by the love of God. Brother Ward then took an offering for me so I could spend the summer in Africa. Believe me, my life took a dramatic turn from that moment!

Within a few months I was in Tanzania, East Africa with missionary Ralph Hagemeier. How that happened was a mystery to me! I had a desire in my heart to serve God and to one day do mission work in Africa, but I seemed to stay in trouble. (Some say preachers' kids are so bad because they hang around with deacons' kids!)

I've often thought I should write a country western song called, "Jesus Loved the Hell out of Me." I don't mean to be crude or irreverent, but that is exactly what happened to me. I like to say: I went to school, and they tried to educate the 'hell' out of me. I went to church, and they tried to preach the 'hell' out of me. I went to jail, and they tried to rehabilitate the 'hell' out of me. I went home, and Dad tried to beat the 'hell' out of me. I went to Jesus, and He loved the 'hell' out of me. I am a living testimony that the love of God is the greatest force on earth.

I AM WHO GOD SAYS I AM

Dad's preaching and Mom's praying and running around the church began to make sense to me. I started studying the scriptures that showed me my redemption in Christ. I began to daily meditated on who I am in Christ. I would say, "I am who God says I am. I have what God says I have. I can do what God says I can do." The power of God's Word started a work in me, and I began to understand my identification with Christ. That's where victory begins — *right where you are!*

Today Mom still runs around the church, which is much larger now. There are a lot more educated and prosperous people in the congregation, but she still says, "Hallelujah! Hallelujah! Hallelujah!" She still shouts "Woooooo!" and runs around the church. The only difference is now I shout and run with her!

> *...I am not ashamed of the gospel of Christ: for it is the power of God unto salvation to every one that believeth...*
>
> **Romans 1:16**

SHOUT IT OUT

The company that makes Shout detergent uses the slogan: "For those tough stains, you have to 'Shout' them out!" I couldn't agree more. Make sure you know what you are shouting about and let it rip!

Smith Wigglesworth said, "Some people would be giants in faith if they just had a shout." Faith shouts while the walls are still standing. He also said, "You need to see how wonderful you are in God and how helpless you are without Him." The truth is, everything changes when you understand who you are in Christ and begin to act like the Bible is true!

Notes:

33

You must have an identity change

to reach your destiny.

Your new identity is

In Christ.

For we are God's (own) handiwork

(His workmanship), recreated in Christ Jesus,

(born anew) that we may do those good works

which God predestined (planned beforehand)

for us, (taking paths which He prepared ahead

of time) that we should walk in them - living

the good life which he prearranged and

made ready for us to live.

Ephesians 2:10, Amplified

5

THE SECRET PLACE

Several years ago, NASA launched a communications satellite. This satellite could not receive or transmit because it was in the wrong orbit; it was absolutely useless. Investors were very concerned because they had already spent $150 million on this project. If the satellite had been operating properly, it would have a potential of a $2 billion profit.

I don't understand much about outer space technology, so that didn't make sense to me. I thought that if you could just get the thing out of this atmosphere and into outer space, it ought to work right. Whether it makes sense to me or not doesn't matter; the thing still wouldn't receive or transmit.

Something had to change for this satellite to receive and transmit. They were able to fire some rockets attached to the sides of the satellite and move it into its proper orbit. As soon as it was moved into place, it began to receive and transmit and its potential was realized.

Finding your place in Christ is the key to receiving from God and transmitting His power. Sometimes you think just because you got born again, everything ought to work right. The new birth is the launching power that gets you into the realm of God; however, there are other changes that must be made in your thinking and speaking that will enable you to receive and transmit the glory of God. You may not be receiving and transmitting because you need to make some adjustments.

MAKING ADJUSTMENTS

Throughout the Bible, we see God moving men and women into the proper orbit to be used by Him. You can see this in the life of Abraham. Abraham had to do some *moving* or make some adjustments so he could receive and transmit. God is constantly working with people to change their thinking, speaking, and acting to open up the miraculous for them.

> God is showing you your place in Christ and setting you in your place for world harvest.

You need to get in the right orbit to receive and transmit. Not only do you need to be in the right place, but God also needs you to be in your place to do His will. He is working in you both to will and to do of His good pleasure (Philippians 2:13). You must be aware of what time it is. God is showing you your place in

Christ and setting you in your place for world harvest.

God wants to bless you; He wants to make you a blessing. He has some "rockets" to help you move into position to see His glory. He has given His Word, the Holy Spirit, and the five-fold ministry gifts to help you make adjustments. It takes some changes to get the glory, and it takes the glory to get some changes. You are being changed so you can fit and function in the proper orbit and realize your potential in Christ.

> When you are born again, you move out of the devil's territory and you are relocated to a new place in Christ.

When you are born again, you move out of the devil's territory and you are relocated to a new place in Christ. You didn't go from being a lost worm to a saved worm! If you are saved, you are in Christ and you are identified with Him. You are raised with Christ and seated together with Him. There is a place by the Father, and that place is in Christ Jesus.

FINDING YOUR PLACE IN THE ROCK

And he said, Thou canst not see my face: for there shall no man see me, and live. And the Lord said, Behold, there is a place by me, and thou shalt stand upon a rock. And it shall come to pass, while my glory passeth by, that I will put thee in a cleft of the rock, and I will cover thee with my hand while I pass by: And I will take away mine hand, and thou shalt see my back parts: but my face shall not be seen.

Exodus 33:20-23

God told Moses, "There is a place by Me for you. You are going to stand on a rock." Moses was getting in on the secret of God's plan of redemption — that man belongs at the right hand of God, meaning *in His presence.*

Even when we were dead in sins, hath quickened us together with Christ (by grace are ye saved;) And hath raised us up together, and made us sit together in heavenly places in Christ Jesus.

Ephesians 2:5,6

Moses was getting in on the secret of the power and authority of God. God told Moses, "There is a place I want to take you. It's right by Me, and you are going to stand upon a rock." Jesus is that rock!

Moses wasn't just going to stand on the rock. God put him in the cleft of the rock, which means, "I'm going to carve out a niche in this rock and put you inside of the rock. Now you can see my glory and my goodness and understand who I AM."

I was raised in church and went to church every time the doors were open. If they had a two-week meeting, we were there every night for two weeks. We never voted on whether or not we would go. My daddy said, "This is not a democracy. This is a dictatorship." We didn't always like it, but I'm glad now that he made us go.

I used to hear the congregation sing, "Rock of Ages, cleft for me, let me hide myself in thee." I never had a clue as to what they were singing about until I was nineteen years old.

When I was nineteen I went to my daddy's church one day and began to pray. After praying in the Holy Ghost for two and a half hours, the Spirit of God fell on me. God spoke to me, "There is a place for you by Me. I want to show you your place." The Lord took me up into the heavenly places in a vision and said, "This is your place." I saw a big rock. God said, "This is your place — right by Me!"

In this vision, God also said to me, "I have had your place by Me reserved for you even before you were born. I prepared it ahead of time. Find that place and get in it. There is deliverance, healing, prosperity, victory, and blessing in that place." In His presence I experienced joy, blessing, and victory like I had never known. I didn't know about Exodus 33 until several years later. God had spoken to me exactly what He spoke to Moses: "...There is a place by me, and thou shalt stand upon a rock," Exodus 33:21.

GLORY! GOD IS ALL GOOD

The prayer of Moses in Exodus 33:18 expresses the desire of every believer. Moses asked God, "Show me thy glory." God responded with, "I will make all my goodness pass before thee." The glory of God is the goodness of God; the goodness of God is a manifestation of the glory of God. God is a good God!

Can you imagine what it would be like to have *all* God's goodness pass before you? That is exactly what happened to Moses — God revealed His goodness to him. The length, depth, breadth, and height of God's goodness overwhelmed Moses — he had an experience with the glory of God. After that day, he was a changed man. The glory of God always changes us. Paul said that the goodness of God leads us to repentance (Romans 2:4). On the road to Damascus, Paul had an experience with the glory of God. The glory so radically changed his life that he had to change his name. Paul was a different man from that day on.

The glory of God so changed Moses' whole countenance that his face radiated — his face was shining. The glory of God got in his skin. The goodness of God changes everything. The glory of God touches and affects every aspect of your life.

Oh, how great is thy goodness...

Psalm 31:19

For how great is his goodness...

Zechariah 9:17

The psalmist David was trying to express the greatness of God's goodness in Psalm 31:19. I like David Baron's commentary on Zechariah 9:17, "Goodness is that attribute of God whereby He loveth to communicate to all who can or will receive it, ALL GOOD — yea Himself, who is the fullness and universality of good, creator of all good, not in one way, not in one kind of goodness only, but absolutely, without beginning, without limit, without measure. This good, His goodness bestoweth on all and each, according to the capacity of each to receive it; nor is there any limit to His giving, save His creature's capacity of receiving."

IN THE ROCK

The only limit to the goodness of God is our capacity to receive. God told Moses, "I will show you my glory...there is a place by me." When believers take their place in Christ they are properly positioned to see the glory of God. That is the observation tower from which we receive.

...there is a place by me, and thou shalt stand upon a rock.

Exodus 33:21

He will put you IN THE ROCK! We now know that rock is Jesus Christ. That is the ROCK OF AGES cleft for me. That is the hiding place, the viewing place and the glory place. Take

Through the power of the death, burial, and resurrection God put us IN CHRIST.

your place in Christ. That is the unlimited receiving place. Through the power of the death, burial, and resurrection, God put us in Christ — in the rock. There is a place by the Father God for every believer. By faith in the precious blood of Jesus, take your place by the Father and receive His goodness!

YOUR PLACE BY THE FATHER

He that dwelleth in the secret place of the most High shall abide under the shadow of the Almighty. I will say of the Lord, He is my refuge and my fortress: my God; in him will I trust.

Psalm 91:1,2

Psalm 91 is a great insurance policy! The company will never go broke. We are to live in that secret place. Find your place by the Father. Live in that place. Don't let Hollywood tell you who you are, where your place is, and how to dress, look, or act. Don't let people shape you. Get in the presence of God and let Him shape you.

Thou art my hiding place; thou shalt preserve me from trouble; thou shalt compass me about with songs of deliverance.

Psalm 32:7

Climb into the secret place by the Father, and you will hear somebody singing songs of deliverance. Hallelujah!

YOUR PLACE IN CHRIST

When Saul met Jesus on the road to Damascus, the first thing he said to Jesus was, "Who art thou, Lord?" (Acts 9:5). The second thing he said to Jesus was, "Lord, what wilt thou have me to do?" (v. 6). Saul, who became Paul, then spent the rest of his life finding out who Jesus was and doing what Jesus wanted him to do. Paul coined a phrase that is the signature of his letters — in Christ.

EVERYBODY ON THE FRONT ROW

The Apostle Paul used the phrase in Christ, in Him, and in Whom over 130 times. God sees you in Christ, but you must see yourself in Him. You are a new creature in Christ. In Him, you are righteous now, blessed now, healed now, free now,

Take your place in Christ and get ready for a front-row seat for the glory of God!

forgiven now, and victorious now! Take your place in Christ and get ready for a front-row seat for the glory of God! Experiencing the glory and goodness of God is not just for a select few believers. God has a reserved seat for you with your name on it!

He is the Lord our Provider, Healer, Shepherd, Righteousness, and Victory!

Very seldom do people use this phrase, *in Christ,* but Paul said in Christ you are a new creation. In Him you are the righteousness of God. In Him you are triumphant. In Him you are blessed. In Him you are redeemed. In Him you have a heritage — an identity and an inheritance!

> *But we all with open face beholding as in a mirror the glory of the Lord, are changed into the same image from glory to glory, even as by the Spirit of the Lord.*
> *2 Corinthians 3:18*

You will look a lot better in Christ than you do outside of Him. So what do you need to do? Get on the rock, climb into the rock, and in Him the glory of God will pass by. In Him you will be changed. In Him is revelation. In Him the goodness of God will come to your house.

I will proclaim the name of the Lord before thee.

Exodus 33:19

I will announce to you the meaning of my name.

The Living Bible

...and so manifest to you what the Eternal is.

Moffat's

The glory is a place of revelation. God reveals Himself to us in ever increasing ways in the glory. He is the Lord our Provider, Healer, Shepherd, Righteousness, and Victory. He is everything we will ever need!

After Moses saw the glory of God, his understanding expanded of who God is and how great His goodness is. Now Moses could receive what was necessary for him to do all that God required of him. We must see the glory of God to do the will of God.

If you are outside of Jesus Christ, and you want to be in Him, pray with me right now: *Father, I want to find my place in Christ by You, which You ordained for me before I was formed in the womb. I acknowledge Jesus Christ as your Son, and I believe He was crucified, buried, resurrected, and ascended to your right hand, Father, paying for my redemption, liberty, health, prosperity, and eternal life with His shed blood. I renounce every work of darkness, and I receive You now, Jesus, as my personal Lord and Savior. Thank You for empowering me with your Spirit, Who will teach, guide, and lead me into my place in You. Amen.*

Notes:

IN CHRIST

you are not just a different

person, you are a

NEW KIND

of person IN HIM.

You are a

NEW KIND

of creature that never

existed before.

Therefore if any man be in Christ, he is a new

creature: old things are passed away;

behold, all things are become new.

II Corinthians 5:17, KJV

6

CHAPTER SIX :

UNDERSTANDING REDEMPTION

Redemption is an accomplished fact in Christ. Jesus said, "You shall know the truth and the truth shall make you free," John 8:32. The truth will not help you if you do not *know* it. You must see what God has done for you. In John 16:13, Jesus called the Holy Spirit the Spirit of Truth. God wants you to be free. He has given you His Holy Spirit to show you the things of Christ.

GOD'S MASTERPIECE

God's masterpiece happened in Christ. What God did for us in the death, burial, and resurrection of Christ is the masterpiece. This is the greatest display of love, wisdom, power, and righteousness in the history of time and eternity. God did in Christ what He wanted to do in every man. You must see what happened from the cross to the throne. God deposited all that He has in Christ and then He put you in Christ.

The Louvre in Paris, France is famous for its display of the world's greatest art collection. It covers more than 40 acres and exhibits many of the world's greatest art treasures. The Louvre has about eight miles of galleries and contains more than a million works of art.

While preaching in Paris, I had one day to do some sightseeing. On the way to the Louvre, my minister friend told me that there were more than 400,000 masterpieces to see. If I spent four seconds in front of each one, it would take me three months to go through the Louvre. Since I did not have that much time, I headed straight for the information desk to find Leonardo da Vinci's world-famous masterpiece, *Mona Lisa*. We headed right for the *Mona Lisa* and spent extra time there.

If you see all the other paintings and sculptures and miss the *Mona Lisa*, you have missed the most important work of art. The same is true of the Bible. It contains the world's greatest collection of God's works of art. However, if you see all the beautiful pictures in the Word of God and miss God's greatest masterpiece, then you have really missed the Bible.

The Bible is the story of man's redemption. All 66 books contain pictures of God's plan and purpose to restore man to Himself. Jesus can be found in every book of the Bible. The Bible is about Jesus, our Redeemer, and His work. The Holy Spirit is your tour guide as you study redemption.

FIRST IMPORTANCE

For I delivered unto you first of all that which I also received, how that Christ died for our sins according to the Scriptures; and that he was buried, and that he rose again the third day according to the Scriptures.

1 Corinthians 15:3,4

The death, burial, and resurrection of Jesus are the center of the Gospel. Paul says, "First of all I delivered unto you...." *The Revised Standard Version* translates this, "as of first importance." *The New English Bible* says, "First and foremost, I handed on to you the facts which had been imparted to me." Weymouth's translation says, "Before all else." The matter of first importance is what God did for us in Christ Jesus in the great plan of redemption.

> The death, burial, and resurrection of Jesus are the center of the Gospel.

Freedom through the payment of a price is the simple definition of redemption. Webster's Dictionary defines the word "redeem" as: *to buy back; to repurchase; to get back; to recover; to ransom; to pay off (a mortgage or note); to liberate from captivity; to deliver; to reclaim.*

Who gave Himself a ransom for all, to be testified in due time.

1 Timothy 2:6

Who gave Himself as the price of freedom for all men...

Plain English

...gave Himself as a ransom payment for all sorts of persons.

Adams

He gave Himself to set all men free. Jesus gave Himself as our ransom payment. He purchased our freedom.

Translator's

Faith begins by knowing redemption facts. God paid the price for you in Christ 2,000 years ago. As the old Gospel song says, "Jesus paid it all." Christianity does not begin with something you do, but with something that has been done for you in Christ. Everything Jesus did in His death and resurrection was done for you, or as some translations say, "in your behalf."

> Christianity does not begin with something you do, but with something that has been done for you in Christ.

If everything Jesus did was for you, it is set to the credit of your account. You could say Jesus gets the *glory* for everything that has been done, but you get the *credit* because He was acting in your behalf.

> *Neither by the blood of goats and calves, but by his own blood, he entered once into the Holy Place, having obtained eternal redemption for us.*
>
> *Hebrews 9:12*

> *...secured our permanent deliverance.*
>
> *Goodspeed*

I like that! Think about it! Jesus has secured our permanent deliverance. That is a powerful statement!

Satan's dominion has been broken over mankind permanently because of what Christ has done. Redemption is not a temporary thing that must be added to by man or replaced later by something more effective. *The Amplified Bible* says, "...a complete redemption, an everlasting release." A complete redemption covers everything. An everlasting release means it lasts forever. God has left nothing out.

All that man needs is supplied in Christ. The past, present, and future have been taken care of. The spirit, soul, and the body have been taken care of — all because of what Jesus has done for us. That means you are not trying to get it or struggling to get it. Jesus got it for you, so it is yours. You have it now. Redemption is an accomplished fact in Christ.

The definition of redemption is deliverance through the payment of a price. Jesus paid the price for your release. Let's look at several *hath* scriptures that the Apostle Paul wrote in his letters. Christ 'hath' redeemed you from the curse of the law (Galatians 3:13). God 'hath' qualified you for your inheritance (Colossians 1:12). He 'hath' delivered you from the power of darkness and 'hath' translated you into the kingdom of His dear Son (Colossians 1:13). He 'hath' blessed you with every spiritual blessing in Christ (Ephesians 1:3). These *hath* scriptures show that Jesus *hath* — past tense — paid the price, and the prisoner must be released.

Man is literally held captive by sin, Satan, sickness, fear, poverty, guilt, and many other things. Jesus paid the price for your freedom. Jesus said that you shall know the truth and the truth shall make you free. He whom the Son sets free is free indeed (John 8:32,36).

In the first message Jesus preached, He said He would "preach deliverance to the captives," Luke 4:18. *Beck's* translation says, "...he sent me to announce to prisoners, 'You are free.'"

Jesus is not talking about His jail ministry. There are a

lot of people who are prisoners who are not in a county jail or a federal prison. A prison ministry is a great ministry, but there are many people held captive who are not behind *steel* bars; they are behind *real* bars.

Only Jesus can bring deliverance. Only the power of the Gospel can bring freedom. Your release from prison has been accomplished through a price that was paid *in your behalf.* In other words, this is not an illegal jail break! Your redemption was legally purchased through the blood of Jesus. His death and resurrection have established a new, universal fact for every man. Jesus purchased your freedom. That means the prison doors of Satan, sin, and sickness are open and the prisoner is free — legally! The prisoner does not have to sneak out some dark night. He can walk out in the daylight because he has a legal release. God has not given you an illegal redemption. God is righteous and He has righteously effected your release.

You were prisoners, but now you are free. You do not have to hide or sneak around the rest of your lives in fear. You have been released, made righteous, and given eternal life — all legally.

You were not redeemed with silver and gold...but with the precious blood of Christ...
1 Peter 1:18,19

No amount of money could buy your release from Satan, sin, or the past. Only the blood of Jesus was legal payment for your freedom. If Jesus paid so high a price for your release, you should not remain behind bars. The prison door is open. You can simply walk out when you see what God, in Christ, has done for you.

A LEGAL RELEASE

It is not like you were prisoners and someone visited you and gave you a file, a little saw, or something else that you could use to try to get out on your own effort. Night after night you would stay up late and secretly file away on the steel bars, hoping not to get caught. After months and years of work, you would finally break a few bars and try to get away. You would run, and the dogs and the guards would chase you as you ran through the swamp, only to be captured again and returned to the same old prison.

> Only the blood of Jesus was legal payment for your freedom.

That is not a picture of God's release! That is the struggle of man's programs to try to get free. The Gospel of Christ is the power of God. God has released you by His power working in Christ in your behalf. The prison door is open! No filing - no sneaking - no running - no swamps - no dogs. It is not your effort. It is God's gift to every man in Christ. Christ "hath" redeemed you. You can walk out of your bondage into glorious liberty. You are legally released. Hold your head up high and boldly walk out in Jesus' name!

YOU ARE REDEEMED

Christ hath redeemed us from the curse of the law, being made a curse for us: for it is written, cursed is everyone that hangeth on a tree.

Galatians 3:13

The law put a curse on us. But Christ took away that curse. He changed places with you. Christ put himself under that curse...

Deaf

Christ it was who redeemed us from that curse of the law, by receiving our curse on his own person.

Hayman's

Christ has purchased our freedom.

Weymouth's

There are three simple, yet powerful statements made in Galatians 3:13. Let's take a closer look. The first fact is that you are redeemed. The second is what you are redeemed from — the curse of the law. The third is what you were redeemed by

— Christ was made a curse for you. In other words, Christ took your curse so you could go free.

Jesus paid much too high a price for your freedom for you to stay bound. It is an insult to God for you to stay in prison when Jesus paid the price for your release. Satan cannot hold you. Sin cannot hold you. The past cannot hold you. Back to our first fact: YOU ARE REDEEMED!

Next Paul tells you what you are redeemed from — the curse of the law (Galatians 3:13). It is true that you will one day go to heaven, and that will be a great day. However, someone said, "I don't just need help in the sweet-by-and-by; I need help in the nasty now-and-now." The curse of the law is broken today for any man or woman who is in Christ. The center of the Gospel is

> It is an insult to God for you to stay in prison when Jesus paid the price for your release.

what God has done for you in Christ. Christ *hath* redeemed you —not just when you get to heaven. The curse of the law has been broken — not for just a few select individuals — for "whosoever" will hear and believe in the Gospel.

Jesus demonstrated this Gospel by healing the sick and setting the captives free in this world. This same Gospel produced the same results in the book of Acts. Romans 10:17 says, "Faith cometh by hearing and hearing by the Word of God." Paul preached the Gospel, and the crippled man at Lystra received faith to be healed as he heard the message (Acts 14:7). Paul said with a loud voice, "Stand upright on thy feet." The man leaped and walked. The people thought Paul healed the man, but it was simply the demonstration of the power of the Gospel.

To see what the curse of the law is you need to turn to Deuteronomy 28:15-68. This list includes everything from sickness and poverty to disaster in the family and the nation. The curse includes everywhere you go, everything you do, and everybody you are with. Under the curse you are a traveling, contagious disaster spiritually, mentally, and physically. But Christ *hath* redeemed you from that curse. He paid the price for your freedom. Even now the curse is broken.

You can see the reverse of the curse by reading Deuteronomy 28:1-13. All these blessings shall come on you and overtake you. You are blessed in the city, field, family, body, business, and you are "the head and not the tail, above only and not beneath."

Christ *hath* redeemed you. The Gospel is the good news that man has been given eternal life

> The Gospel is the good news that man has been given eternal life through Jesus Christ.

through Jesus Christ. That life is the very life of God imparted to His children. It is overcoming life - reigning life - victorious life - blessing life - healing life - not just for when you get to heaven. It is heaven's life flowing in you in this world.

The Gospel of Christ is the power of God unto salvation to everyone who believes (Romans 1:16). Someone said that if you think you need more power, you really just need more Gospel. The Gospel is the power of God. The word "gospel" means *glad tidings* or *good news*. The Gospel is where God has released His power for the purpose of producing salvation.

God has targeted His power at man's deepest needs — spirit, soul, and body. God knows the root of your problems, and He has effectually focused His power there. Everything Satan has done in Adam, God has reversed in Christ. The word "salvation" has a five-fold meaning: deliverance, healing, safety, preservation, and soundness. This is not just a "heaven" message; it is an "earth" message as well. It is not just something for later; this is a NOW message. Notice we have redemption in Christ.

> **In whom we have redemption through his blood even the forgiveness of sins.**
>
> **Colossians 1:14**

> **...who bought our freedom with his own blood.**
>
> **Living Bible**

> **... by whom we have been ransomed from captivity.**
>
> **Goodspeed**

In whom we have redemption through his blood, the forgiveness of sins, according to the riches of his grace.

Ephesians 1:7

It is in and through Christ and the sacrifice of His life that we have been liberated....

Barclay

...through the shedding of His blood we possess freedom in Him....

Barth

For it was by this one's supreme sacrifice that we got our 'emancipation'....

Jordan

...who bought us with his blood to forgive our sins and set us free

Beck

THE CENTER OF THE GOSPEL

The center of the Gospel is the death, burial, and resurrection of Christ. After His resurrection, Jesus told the disciples, "Go into all the world and preach the Gospel to every creature," Mark 16:15.

There are ten messages recorded in the book of Acts that show us what they understood the Gospel to be — five messages by the apostle Peter and five by the apostle Paul. In each of these messages, the central point is that Jesus died and was buried, but He arose from the dead. He is alive! This is the center of the Gospel. The disciples knew what those events had produced for every man. The power that God released in the resurrection of Christ is contained in the message.

Someone said that the death, burial, and resurrection of Christ are eternal God events. We give them a date and place because they are historical events, but they are more than just history. They are supernatural, eternal God events, and they can be visited at any point in time as though they were happening right then. The same power that God released in these events is in the message. The Gospel contains the power that God released in Christ 2,000 years ago.

The Gospel contains the power that God released in Christ 2,000 years ago.

The Gospel produces faith. The Word of God is a living thing. Christ *hath* redeemed you! The Gospel is not the good news that God *can* help you. It is not the good news that God *wants* to help you. It is the good news that God has already helped you in Christ. The price has been paid, and the prisoner is free. The curse of sin and Satan has been broken by the mighty name of Jesus. His blood still speaks of your redemption today.

PAUL'S SYSTEM OF TRUTH

In the Apostle Paul's letters to the church, there is a network of revelation concerning who Christ is and what He has done. I call it "Paul's System of Truth" from *Weymouth's* translation of Romans 6:17, "But thanks be to God that though you were once in thralldom to sin, you have now yielded a hearty obedience to that system of truth in which you have been instructed."

This system of truth can be found throughout Paul's letters. These things are interrelated and form a redemption network centered on the death and resurrection of Christ with the restoration of man as the object. There are eight points in Paul's system of truth.

1. Man on three dimensions: spirit, soul, and body
2. Identification with Adam
3. Man's condition in Adam
4. What happened to Jesus from the cross to the throne
5. Identification with Christ
6. Who we are and what we have NOW in Christ
7. What Jesus is doing for us at the right hand of God
8. How to develop to spiritual maturity

I have studied Paul's system of truth since I was about seventeen years old. I still do not tire of it and have never completed it. I will only touch on this briefly here.

> *But God be thanked, that ye were the servants of sin, but you have obeyed from the heart that form of doctrine which was delivered you. And being then made free from sin, you became the servants of righteousness.*
>
> *Romans 6:17*

Not only are you free from sin, but here it says that you became a servant or a slave of righteousness. How did that happen? Paul says "You obeyed the form of doctrine that was delivered you."

Many people say, "Well, doctrine is legalism, or doctrine is denominationalism, or doctrine is going to lock me in." However, the Apostle Paul says, "All scripture is given by inspiration of God, and is profitable for instruction in righteousness: That the man of God may be perfect," 2 Timothy 3:16,17.

Weymouth's translation of Romans 6:17 says, "You obeyed the system of truth in which you were instructed in." So doctrine is a system of truth. What is a system? A system is a group of items that are interrelated and interdependent. They cannot stand alone; they must work together. That is a system.

Networks work together. For example, television networks such as ABC, NBC, and CBS have affiliates. You must show the same programs on your affiliate station as they show or you cannot be in their network. Computer systems have networks. The universe has a solar system. The human body has a nervous system and a digestive system.

The simplest illustration of a system is a chain. A chain is a group of links that are interdependent upon each other for the strength of the whole. Not any one link can be a chain; all the links are dependent upon each other. In Paul's system of truth the eight points are the eight links which center on redemption.

Whatever Paul taught in Rome, he also taught in Colossae, Ephesus, Corinth, Thessalonica, and wrote in his letter to the Hebrews. This system of truth contains the revelation of what God did in Christ in His death, burial, and resurrection and its effect on you. This is something Paul covers more thoroughly than the other Bible writers.

PROCLAMATION, DEMONSTRATION, EXPLANATION

The four Gospels - Matthew, Mark, Luke, and John - are a proclamation of the Gospel. The book of Acts is a demonstration of the Gospel. Paul's epistles are an explanation of the Gospel. We must have the Gospel of Christ in all three forms: proclamation, demonstration, and explanation.

One of the Apostle Paul's assignments was to write a Holy Spirit-inspired explanation of the Gospel of Christ. Paul's revelation tells us the necessity of the crucifixion of Christ. He tells us what happened in the unseen, or *in the spirit*. The four Gospels tell what man saw and Paul's epistles tell us what God saw. Paul tells us what happened in God's economy when Jesus died and was raised from the dead. Paul tells what happened when Jesus ascended into heaven and secured our redemption with His blood.

The four Gospels are a photograph of redemption — Paul's epistles are an X-ray. You can see things in an X-ray of an individual that you cannot see in a photograph. Both of these pictures are necessary. The Gospel is multifaceted and meets every need.

> The four Gospels are a photograph of redemption — Paul's epistles are an X-ray.

Notes:

God would not make an

"unrighteous" new creature.

He already has an unrighteous old

creature. As a new creature

IN CHRIST

you have been made the

righteousness of God

IN HIM.

...in our behalf God identified Him with

everything in the whole realm of sin in order

that by trusting Him, we might become

(recipients of) God's kind of righteousness.

2 Corinthians 5:21 (Black.)

7

IN CHRIST DETERMINISM

If you have studied psychology, you know three factors have determined what kind of person you are: genetic determinism, psychic determinism, and environmental determinism. The reason it is called *determinism* is because there is no escape.

There is some truth to all these things, but God brings another factor, which I call *in Christ* determinism.

> *...if any man be IN CHRIST, he is a new creature: old things are passed away; behold all things are become new.*
>
> *2 Corinthians 5:17*

Genetic determinism means you are what you are because of your genes. You are what you are because of your parents or what runs in your family. Being in Christ has given you a gene change. That means you have been regenerated or re-gened. God has done some genetic engineering in Christ. You have been born of God. God is your Father, Jesus is your older brother, and some new things run in your family.

Once you are in Christ and in the body of Christ, there are supernatural connections all around you.

Psychic determinism means that your identity, your behavior, and your potential are produced by your thinking. Although there is some truth to that, you have some new thoughts now. God said, "I will give you My thoughts now, so have another determinism."

I like what a friend of mine said, "I carry my brains in my hand. When someone asks me what I think, I say, 'Hold it just a second. Let me look in my brains.'" Then he would open his Bible.

When someone asks you what you think about something, say, "Hold it just a minute. I have my brains right here. Let me see what I think. I think I am healed. I think I am happy. I think I am prosperous. I think my steps are ordered by the Lord. That is what I think."

Environmental determinism means you are what you are, and your surroundings and the influences around you limit your future. Once you are in Christ and in the body of Christ, there are supernatural connections all around you. When you go to your company, your church, and start praying, you are in a whole new environment (Acts 4:23).

What makes you the way that you are? Once you get born again, these three determinism factors all change. Your future and your potential are radically altered as a result of it.

People with *in Christ* determinism think God's thoughts and see themselves in Him. In Christ determinism is stronger than any other factor that tries to shape you. There are 130 in Christ, in Him, in Whom, and in the Lord scriptures that show your new identity.

> *...old things are passed away; behold, all things are become new.*
>
> *2 Corinthians 5:17*

> *...the original conditions have passed away...they have been replaced by new conditions.*
>
> *Wade*

> *...a true Christian is not merely a man altered but a man remade.*
>
> *Deane*

The old conditions are gone, and there are new conditions. Everything has become new. It is good news that all things are made new, but it is also good news that old things are passed away. If all you have as a Christian is something new added to you, you would still have to deal with and live with the old conditions. In Christ old things are passed away. Another translation says, "...dead and gone." Your past is dead and gone.

God told Jeremiah, "Go down to the potter's house, and I'll show you how I can take a vessel that has been marred and make it all over again," Jeremiah 18:4. People will look at you and say, "You do not look like the same person." You can say, "I'm not. I am in Christ."

IDENTIFY WITH CHRIST

People often talk about what happened to them in their past. Their identity and identification are so hooked up with their past. Some people even call themselves by an experience that happened to them, such as, "I am divorced." No, divorce might have happened to you, but you are not presently divorced.

Some people identify with what has happened to them. They say, "I was abused." Then they join a support group and their identity gets worse because everybody there is abused.

However, your identification with Christ changes everything. It does not mean that you were not abused, you did not have a problem with drinking, or you were not divorced.

People go through all those things, but your identification with Christ is stronger than that. You could say that what happened to you in Christ is bigger than anything else that has happened to you.

This does not mean your past experience did not happen. The devil is mean, and bad things happen to good people. Sometimes things happen to people when they are children and they never get over it. As a matter of fact, when you start talking to people, what happened when they were 12, 15, or 25 years old will come out of their mouths. Even when they are 70 years old, they still talk about what happened. Someone did something to them that impacted their lives so greatly, they never got beyond it.

> What happened to Christ in His death, burial, and resurrection is greater than anything else that ever happened to you.

Oh, but in Christ! What happened to Christ in His death, burial, and resurrection is greater than anything else that ever happened to you. Hallelujah!

POWERFUL PREPOSITIONS

These important prepositions help us understand our identification with Christ: *for, with, in, by,* and *through.* Arthur S. Way commented in his translation of *The Letters of Saint Paul*:

Prepositions "on," "by," "through," "with" are compelled frequently to do duty for which they are inadequate. What they are intended to express is practically nullified by the fact that they are required to express too much.

In Paul's epistles these prepositions go unnoticed, even though they are the connecting words that show the relationship of the subjects mentioned, in this case the believer's identification with Christ. I agree with Arthur S. Way, and I also would add the preposition *in*, which is used more than 130 times in Paul's letters.

The preposition *for* shows substitution. Christ died *for* us or in our behalf. The preposition *with* shows identification. The preposition *in* shows union with Christ. The preposition *through* shows application. For example:

I can do all things through Christ who strengtheneth me.

Philippians 4:13

The phrase "in Christ" is never translated to mean anything else except "in union with Christ." That is the only other way it can be translated. What does it mean to be in Christ?

JOINED TO CHRIST

"But he that is joined unto the Lord is one spirit," 1 Corinthians 6:17. What does that mean? When you were born again, your spirit was joined to the Master, or joined to Christ. Like a bay of water is one with the ocean, your spirit is one with Christ. When the water rises in the ocean, it rises in the bay. The same *stuff* that is in the ocean gets into the bay. The same *stuff* that is in Christ right now is in you. I am talking about the same *stuff* — the same life, same victory, same joy, and same power.

ACKNOWLEDGE YOUR UNION WITH CHRIST

When you get born again, you get "in Christ-ed." Your spirit is joined to Christ. One translation of 1 Corinthians 6:17 says, "your spirit is joined to the Master." You share a common life, the same life, the same righteousness, the same triumph, and the same blessing. When God looks at you, He sees you in Him, but your faith will not be effectual until you start to acknowledge, confess, and declare your identity in Christ. You have to acknowledge it. Confession is one way to acknowledge your identity in Christ.

> The same stuff that is in Christ right now is in you.

I encourage you to make a daily confession of who you are in Christ. Actually, the Word says to acknowledge it. So acknowledge could mean more than just confession. In other words, you declare it, but to acknowledge it would mean to go ahead and act like it.

That is why people need to run, laugh, dance, shout, and daily rejoice by faith. This demonstrates our victory in Christ.

> Confession is one way to acknowledge your identity in Christ.

That is an acknowledgement of the triumph of Christ. It is an acknowledgement that the victory of Christ is so big that the devil does not have a chance. This is not even a close call. This is a 24-second knockout. Do not hesitate when the Holy Spirit is moving. What He is trying to get you to do is acknowledge who you are in Christ.

The devil is scared of you when you get in the Spirit. When you are in the flesh, thinking of yourself in the natural, you let the devil keep you in the realm of your soul, your reasoning, and your mind. The devil can whip you all day long.

The moment you step out of the natural and out of circumstances, you step right over into who you are in Christ. Your spirit man begins to respond by taking ascendancy over your flesh, your mind, and the circumstances of your faith. Your inner man will rise up and say, "All right, devil, I have had enough of this." The devil will mess with you all day long until you rise up in the Spirit. I like to say it like this: A fly will not land on a hot stove!

I LIKE THAT "AM" BUSINESS

When I was a senior in high school, I found 130 "in Christ" scriptures, wrote them down, and began to confess them. I put them on a cassette tape. Every morning when I woke up, I heard myself saying, "I am a new creation in Christ, old things are passed away, everything has become new."

I like that "I am" business. The world is full of people who are *trying to be* and *used to be*. Have you ever heard somebody say, "He's a wannabe"? "Therefore if any man be in Christ, he IS...," 2 Corinthians 5:17. This is present tense — right now. I am not trying to be, need to be, hope to be, or someday going to be. Right now, I am in Christ. I am in I AM and so I am. I am a new creation. I am the righteousness of God. I am triumphant.

It is not something I am trying to get or something I am trying to do. It is something in my genes. I have been born again, and God's life and nature is in me. It is in my genes; it runs in my family. I am in union with the Champion. I am in Christ.

SUBSTITUTION AND IDENTIFICATION

When we talk about identification with Christ, it is rather difficult to understand. You say, "Identification with Christ — what does that mean?" That is the center of the

Church. It is really the center of all theology.

We are instructed to practice two ordinances in the Church today. One of them is water baptism and the other one is the Lord's Supper. Water baptism is a picture of your identification with Christ in His death, burial, and resurrection (Romans 6:3-6).

The Lord's Supper is to be practiced regularly. Jesus said, "...this do in remembrance of me...this do ye, as oft as ye drink it, in remembrance of me," 1 Corinthians 11:24,25. Eating His flesh and partaking of His blood in the Lord's Supper reveals that you are in union with Him. These are types of your union and your identification with Christ. You are in Him. You are crucified with Him. You are buried with Him, and you are raised up with Him.

BE SWALLOWED UP

Even the mystery which hath been hid from ages and from generations, but now is made manifest to his saints: To whom God would make known what is the riches of the glory of this mystery among the Gentiles; which is Christ in you, the hope of glory.

Colossians 1:26,27

Paul shared his revelation in Colossians 1:26,27, "This mystery was hidden for ages and generations, but I am going to to tell you what the secret is. It is Christ in you, the hope of glory." I am swallowed up in Christ. In other words, man's condition was so bad, he could not be fixed. God had to make a totally brand new man. Your identification with Christ in His death, burial, and resurrection shows your new conditions. In Him you died, you were buried, and you were raised from the dead.

IN CHRIST SURGERY

I heard the story of a California fireman whose hand was burned so badly, the doctors thought they would have to amputate. They decided to try another procedure because of the human body's regenerative powers. They operated on the fireman, inserted his burned hand inside his body, and left it in there. When they removed the hand after a number of days, the skin had begun to grow back again.

God said, "Man's condition is so bad, it looks like he is going to have to be amputated. Before we do that, I have a surgical procedure. I can cut Myself open and I will put him inside of Me." On the cross an incision was made, and God put you in Christ.

You were on your way to death, destruction, poverty, and lack, and God said, "There is nothing we can do. We will have to cut ourselves open and put man in us." Paul called this a mystery, but this is redemption — you are in Him. You are joined to Him, identified with Him, and in Him we live and move and have our being (Acts 17:28).

The surgery God performed in the death, burial, and resurrection of Christ was such a massive project, He planned it for thousands of years. Our redemption was such a big project, He had to talk to people for thousands of years just to get someone to believe Him. Because of man's condition, this "in Christ" surgical procedure was the only way man could be saved. The difference between Christianity and all other religions is this fact: Jesus died, He was buried, and on the third day He arose from the dead.

> The difference between Christianity and all other religions is this fact: Jesus died, He was buried, and on the third day He arose from the dead.

Mankind did not need a book. We did not need a lesson. We needed a new birth. We needed to be redeemed — we needed the blood of Jesus. We needed His death and His resurrection. You cannot just give people a lesson. That is why every other religion is inferior to Christianity. Jesus died, He was buried, and He arose from the dead. That is the center of the Gospel.

Your identification
with Christ is activated
by your identical confession
of faith of who you are
In Christ.

I am crucified with Christ: nevertheless
I live; yet not I, but Christ liveth in me:
and the life which I now live in the
flesh I live by the faith of the Son
of God, Who loved me,
and gave Himself
for me.
Galatians 2:20, KJV

8

UNDERSTANDING RIGHTEOUSNESS

Understanding righteousness and understanding redemption are essential to your faith working mightily. Righteousness simply means "right standing with God." The main theme of the book of Romans is righteousness. The Apostle Paul begins by saying that the Gospel of Christ is fundamentally a revelation of righteousness.

> *For I am not ashamed of the Gospel of Christ;*
> *for it is the power of God unto salvation to every*
> *one that believeth; to the Jew first and also to*
> *the Greek. For therein is the righteousness of*
> *God revealed from faith to faith; as it is written,*
> *The just shall live by faith.*
>
> *Romans 1:16,17*

Righteousness is living in a state of divine favor or being pleasing, accepted, or approved by God. Righteousness is a gift.

For if by one man's offense, death reigned by one; much more they which receive the abundance of grace and the gift of righteousness shall reign in life by one, Jesus Christ.

Romans 5:17

The Gospel is a revelation of how God makes man righteous. 2 Corinthians 5:21 not only tells you what you have but how you got it, "For He hath made Him to be sin for us who knew no sin, that we might be made the righteousness of God in Him." Jesus took your sinful condition so you could receive His righteous condition. He took your place so you could have His place.

> Everything Jesus did, He did for you — it is set to the credit of your account as though you did it.

SUBSTITUTION, IDENTIFICATION, UNION

Everything Jesus did, He did for you — it is set to the credit of your account as though you did it. This is the progression from substitution to identification and union with Christ. When someone is born again, He is a new creature in

Christ Jesus; old things are passed away and everything is new (2 Corinthians 5:17). God would not make an unrighteous new creature. If you are saved, you must be righteous.

> *That if thou shalt confess with thy mouth the Lord Jesus and shalt believe in thine heart that God hath raised Him from the dead, thou shalt be saved. For with the heart man believeth unto righteousness and with the mouth confession is made unto salvation.*
>
> *Romans 10:9,10*

> *Who was delivered for our offenses, and was raised again for our justification.*
>
> *Romans 4:25*

When Jesus was raised from the dead, you were justified or declared righteous. You could say that Jesus was not raised from the dead until you were declared righteous. The penalty for sin was paid in full and God declared you righteous. This is the reason the Gospel is good news to every person.

> *But now the righteousness of God without the law is manifested, being witnessed by the law and the prophets; Even the righteousness of God which is by faith of Jesus Christ unto and upon all them that believe; for there is no*

difference. For all have sinned, and come short of the glory of God; Being justified freely by His grace through the redemption that is in Christ Jesus: Whom God set forth to be a propitiation through faith in His blood, to declare His righteousness for the remission of sins that are past, through the forbearance of God; To declare, I say, at this time his righteousness: that He might be just, and the justifier of him which believeth in Jesus.

Romans 3:21-26

Righteousness is yours through faith in the precious blood of Jesus. God has not only forgiven the sinner, but He has made him His very own righteousness. He has not only forgiven the one who believes in Jesus, but He has forgotten that he has ever done anything wrong (Isaiah 43:25,26). You are not only forgiven, but you have been recreated with God's own righteousness imparted to you. We have been recreated in righteousness.

Jesus has given you His standing with the Father God. Jesus has let you share His place with God. In Christ is your place of righteousness. In Him you are free from the power, control, and effects of sin. In Him you have confidence in the presence of God. In Christ and by faith in His blood, you have boldness not only before God, but also before your adversary, the devil, who comes to accuse you. In Christ you are free from guilt and shame. In Him you are free from inferiority and unworthiness.

You can grow in faith and love and holiness, but not in righteousness. You can never get any more righteous than the moment you are born again and washed in the blood of Jesus. Righteousness is a gift. You are a righteous new creature!

FIRST CLASS RIGHTEOUSNESS

I do a lot of international flying and know that you can fly economy class, business class, or first class. I have had the blessing of flying first class on occasion and have noticed there is a great deal of difference between the service in first class and economy class.

When you come on the plane in first class, immediately the attendant will make sure you have everything to make you comfortable. You are offered something to drink or eat. They will take your coat, make sure you have a blanket or pillow, and help you put up your belongings. However, in economy class they almost act irritated that you are there! The seating isn't so comfortable. Don't ask for anything special — they'll tell you to get it yourself.

If you have an aisle seat, you can look up the aisle and see into first class. You know things are much better up there, but you are stuck in economy class. After a while they won't even let you look. They pull a curtain as if to say you don't even deserve to look into first class! You develop a real economy mentality as the person next to you goes to sleep and snores and slobbers. However, God spoke to me through all of this and said, "There is no *Economy Class righteousness.* All of the God-kind of righteousness is *First Class righteousness!"*

The moment anyone receives Jesus, that man or woman is made the righteousness of God. You are heirs of God and joint-heirs with Christ (Romans 8:17). You reign as kings in life because of God's grace and the gift of righteousness (Romans 5:17). When you come on board in Christ, all heaven stands at attention. The blessings of heaven are yours in Him. The authority of heaven is yours in His name. God is your very own Father and you are His very own child.

The blessings and benefits of righteousness are listed throughout the Old and New Testaments. In Him you have been made the righteousness of God. Understanding righteousness has a mighty effect on every area of your life, including your prayer life.

> *The effectual fervent prayer of a righteous man makes tremendous power available, dynamic in its working.*
>
> *James 5:16, Amplified*

Smith Wigglesworth said, "You need to see how wonderful you are in God and how helpless you are in yourself." You must see yourself in Christ. Without Him, you could do nothing. You have tremendous power in prayer when you abide in Christ and His Words abide in you.

> **You have tremendous power in prayer when you abide in Christ and His Words abide in you.**

If you abide in me and my words abide in you, you shall ask whatever you will and it shall be done unto you.

John 15:7

FREEDOM FROM GUILT AND SIN CONSCIOUSNESS

God does not want His children to live with a continual consciousness of sin, failure, defeat, weakness, guilt, and inferiority. As a father of two children, I know I don't want my children to live that way. God is your heavenly Father and He is glorified when you reflect His life, joy, and victory. This does not mean that you won't have challenges. You live in a world that is full of adversity, but you are overcomers because you are born of God (1 John 5:4). Instead of a sense of sin or guilt, you should have a sense of righteousness and triumph.

Now thanks be unto God, which always causeth
us to triumph in Christ and maketh manifest
the savour of His knowledge by us in every
place.

2 Corinthians 2:14

In Christ is your place of triumph. Notice Paul said "in every place." The savour is the smell of victory. Paul was in some difficult places but he said, "I keep smelling like the victory of Jesus." Paul was shipwrecked, snake-bit, beaten in the head, and left for dead, yet he came out saying, "I am more than a conqueror in Christ," (Romans 8:37). He came out smelling like a rose with victory over the world, the flesh, and the devil. Paul saw himself in Christ.

Some people have been through some very tough things, and they came out smelling like their bad experience. God wants you to keep smelling like the triumph of Christ. This means you have to live in the consciousness and with the confession of who you are in Christ.

THE SMELL OF TRIUMPH

Several years ago on one of our family vacations, I decided to drive through a wild animal park in Oklahoma. We purchased some small buckets of feed to give to the various animals as we drove through. My daughter, Alicia, was sitting in the front passenger seat. My wife, Trina, and my son, Aaron, were sitting in the back seat.

At first all we saw were deer, so we fed the deer and they were nice and cute. Then a llama came strolling up on Alicia's side of the van. He scared her so much that she quickly pushed the power switch and rolled up her window.

I laughed and said, "I'm not afraid of a llama." The llama must have heard me say that because immediately he came to my side of the van. I began to feed him out of my bucket. All of a sudden he forced his whole head in the window and ate out of my bucket with his whole head in my lap. Alicia and I began to laugh nervously. The llama pulled his head out of the bucket and sneezed in my van! Llama spit and snot and slimy stuff went all across the front dash and on our clothes. It was nasty and had a terrible smell. I immediately slapped the llama's head to get him out and rolled up the window, but the damage had been done.

We left the park and headed for the nearest store to get something to clean up the mess. We finally got the slime out, but the smell was more difficult. During our whole vacation we could smell the llama sneeze every time we got in the van. That smell stayed in the van for months before we finally got it out. The llama was gone, but the smell was still there!

Sin and Satan are the same way. When the devil gets his head in your life, he will not leave until he has sneezed on you and made a mess. Jesus shed His blood, died, and arose from the dead for you to undo all that the devil has done. God not only wants to get the devil's head out and clean up the mess, but He also wants you to be free from the smell of the past. God does not want you to smell like sin, failure, guilt, and shame.

God wants you to apply the blood of Jesus to your life in every situation and smell like the triumph of Christ.

But if we walk in the light, as he is in the light, we have fellowship one with another and the blood of Jesus Christ his son cleanseth us from all sin.

1 John 1:7

If we confess our sins, He is faithful and just to forgive us our sins and to cleanse us from all unrighteousness.

1 John 1:9

In whom we have boldness and access with confidence by the faith of him.

Ephesians 3:12

God wants you to apply the blood of Jesus to your life in every situation and smell like the triumph of Christ. In Christ you have a sense of righteousness and victory. You can forget about the past and press on for the high calling of God today and in your future (Philippians 3:13-14). The blood of Jesus cleanses us from all sin. Thank God for the Blood of Jesus.

You don't need more POWER;

You need more GOSPEL.

The GOSPEL of Christ

is the power of God.

The same power that is in the

actual event of the death, burial,

and resurrection is in the

message of the Gospel.

For I am not ashamed of the gospel of Christ:

for it is the power of God unto salvation to

everyone that believeth; to the Jew first,

also to the Greek.

Romans 1:16, KJV

9

YOUR IDENTIFICATION WITH CHRIST

I have been crucified with Christ and I no longer live, but Christ lives in me. The life I live in the body, I live by faith in the Son of God, who loved me and gave himself for me.

Galatians 2:20, NIV

The substitutionary work of Christ and His love for you is revealed in Galatians 2:20. Paul's understanding of Christianity is based on substitution (what Christ has done for you) and on identification (that Jesus took your place and died your death so that you might live). Everything Jesus did, He did for you. It is set to the credit of your account as though you did it.

> Everything Jesus did, He did for you. It is set to the credit of your account as though you did it.

Jesus gave Himself for you; He died in your place. Now you can see how God changes your identity.

AN IDENTITY CHANGE

Paul is not talking about a spiritual state that he has come to. Rather, he is talking about what happened on the cross in the death, burial, and resurrection of Christ — what happened the moment he accepted Jesus as his Lord and Savior. Paul is talking about an identity change. The moment you say yes to Jesus — not some thirty years later — you can say, "I was crucified with Christ: nevertheless I live; yet not I, but Christ lives in me," Galatians 2:20. The Noli translation says, "I have been crucified with Christ. Now it is not my old self, but Christ Himself lives in me."

To be crucified with Christ means the old self, the old person you used to be, is gone and now Christ Himself lives in you. You ought to be doing very well if Christ Himself is living in you! He has conquered the devil, the world, and the flesh. He is triumphant!

You can get real mental about this and say, "I wonder what he is trying to say?" If you think too much about it, you will never figure it out. Accept it at face value and declare, "This is God's revelation of Christianity. It is who I am and what I have. I have been crucified with Christ. Christ Himself now lives in me." Hallelujah!

I died when Christ died on the cross. I do not live now, but Christ lives in me.

Galatians 2:20, Cressman

I have been crucified with Christ and live now not with my own life but with the life of Christ who lives in me. The life I now live in this body, I live in faith — faith in the Son of God who loved me and sacrificed Himself for my sake.

Jerusalem

Recently, after I taught a class about identification with Christ, someone said to me, "Pastor, all the sermons I have ever heard about what happened on the cross always identified us with the crowd — the Roman soldiers, Mary the mother of Jesus, the disciples, or someone in the crowd who was hollering, 'Crucify Him.' No one ever told us that Jesus identified with us and we are identified with Him."

Christ took me to the cross with Him and I died there with Him.

Galatians 2:20, Laubach

That means you were crucified together with Him when He was crucified. This is the most powerful aspect of your redemption. If you died with Him, Paul says, we were made alive, raised, and seated with Him (Ephesians 2:4-6).

WERE YOU THERE?

The old Gospel hymn says, "Were you there when they crucified my Lord? Were you there when they laid Him in the tomb? Were you there when he rose up from the grave?

> More happened on the cross and in the resurrection than can be seen with the natural eye.

Sometimes it causes me to tremble...." I remember hearing that song as a child and thinking, "Of course I wasn't there. That happened 2,000 years ago." I did not understand Paul's revelation. I did not understand what happened "in the Spirit" or what God saw happen in the death, burial, and resurrection of Christ.

The Holy Spirit through the Apostle Paul says that we were there in the death, burial, resurrection, triumph, and seating of Jesus Christ. More happened on the cross and in the resurrection than can be seen with the natural eye. Jesus took you with Him in his death, burial, and resurrection — that is the X-ray picture. That is what God saw. When you see what God saw, it will make you tremble sometimes. The power and the glory of God are yours in Christ.

THE GOSPEL IS A GROUP PICTURE

The first thing you look for in a group picture is yourself. Since the Gospel is a group picture, you need to look for yourself and by faith find yourself in the death, burial, and resurrection of Christ. You don't look too good on the cross, but in the resurrection you look great in Christ.

WHAT HAPPENED AT THE CROSS

Sometimes even theologians and historians struggle with scripture that talks about our identity with Christ. They say, "The Apostle Paul is kind of a 'loony toon' because he says he was crucified with Christ. We know Paul was not crucified with Christ because he was not even in Jerusalem when Jesus was crucified." They might even say, "So how could he have been crucified with Christ? Jesus was on the center cross. There was a thief on one side and a criminal on the other. How could Paul say he was crucified with Christ?" I believe Paul was talking about revelation knowledge of what happened in the Spirit when Jesus was crucified, buried, and resurrected.

> Since the Gospel is a group picture, you need to look for yourself and by faith find yourself in the death, burial, and resurrection of Christ.

You can approach what happened on the cross with a

sentimental view; however, it will not cause a change in your identity. For example, people may cry or get goose bumps while watching a drama of the cross and the resurrection of Christ, but give them three days and they will be back in the bar. When there is no change in identity, they will go right back into sin.

If you really want to strike at the root of your old sinful nature and have an identity change, there must be revelation knowledge of what happened in the death, burial, and resurrection of Christ — not just a sentimental or ceremonial view. People can believe an innocent man died, but that is not the real view of the cross. Jesus was innocent. He knew no sin and He was made to be sin for us. It was not the Roman soldiers who crucified Him because Jesus said, "...I lay down my life, that I might take it again. No man taketh it from me, but I lay it down of myself...," John 10:17,18.

JESUS TOOK US WITH HIM

You may be asking, "What took Jesus to the cross, then?" It wasn't the Roman soldiers. It wasn't even the Jews. What really took Christ to the cross was the need for Him to take you and me with Him. In other words, it was planned ahead of time. Jesus was made to be sin for us. He took our sin. We died there with Him! Don't get mad at any group of people for Jesus' crucifixion. Instead, get mad at sin and the devil and recognize what God did for you in Jesus' death, burial, and resurrection.

Notes:

The reason a man

in Christ

is something that never

existed before is because

Jesus, in His death, burial,

and resurrection, did something

that had never been

done before.

...and a true Christian is not merely a man

altered, but a man remade...

2 Corinthians 5:17, Deane

10

JESUS IN YOUR JERSEY

He that spared not his own Son, but delivered him up for us all, how shall he not with him also freely give us all things?

Romans 8:32

How, then, shall we respond to all this? If God is rootin' for us, who can win over us? If he didn't hold back his own Son, but put him in the game for us all, won't he even more gladly, in addition to his Son, equip us with all we need to win the game?

Jordan

I played football in high school so I know what it means to come in as a substitute for somebody. If you have ever watched a football game on TV, you hear announcers giving their commentary on what is taking place in the game. You may hear the announcer talk about a particular player, let's say number 65 (that was my number in high school). The guys on the other team are pounding him all over the field and stomping him really bad. He is bleeding and has grass stains and dirt all over him. Every time the ball is hiked, number 65 gets slaughtered. He gets pushed so far back that you think he's on the other team. Number 65 is just being dominated by the other team. Then the coach says, "I've got a plan." He pulls number 65 out and replaces him with the strongest man on the team.

GOD'S GOT A PLAN

That's what God did for us when He sent Jesus to die in our place. God put Jesus in number 65's (mankind's) jersey. Number 65 runs back on the field, and now the whole picture changes. The announcer says, "You know, something has happened to number 65. He's moving that ball all over the field now."

> God moved on the inside of you and got in your jersey. He identified with you so you could identify with Him.

Before man was identified with Christ in His death, burial, and resurrection, he had been whipped all over by depression, discouragement, fear, failure, shame, and guilt. But now, number 65 is winning and he's dominating.

God saw our condition and knew that He could not train us enough to change the game. He knew there was no other way than to get in our jersey. He said, "We can't train them, let's just jump on the inside of them. I'll live on the inside of them. I'll walk in them." God moved on the inside of you and got in your jersey. He identified with you so you could identify with Him.

I am crucified with Christ: nevertheless I live; yet not I, but Christ liveth in me: and the life which I now live in the flesh I live by the faith of the Son of God, who loved me, and gave himself for me.

Galatians 2:20

Identification is defined in Webster's Dictionary as: *to consider or treat as the same, the condition or fact of being, the same in all qualities under consideration.* These words are all related to each other: identification, identity, identical, and identified. Many people live and die and never really find their true identity.

PROOF OF IDENTIFICATION

Have you ever checked in for a flight and been asked for proof of identification? You can say, "Here I am. Can't you see - this is me? I can prove that I exist. Just look." Even when I played baseball in elementary school, they wanted to see my birth certificate! I could have said, "Look, I can prove I was born. Here I am." That was not enough. I needed some authentic, legal, official proof that I was who I said I was. This is all a part of life in this natural world.

In the realm of the Spirit you say, "Well, here I am. Obviously, I am who I am." God will ask, "Do you have any identification on you?" You say, "I sure do, I have some identification right here in Galatians 2:20: I am crucified with Christ: nevertheless I live; yet not I but Christ liveth in me."

Notes:

There is a radical change

in Christ.

Everything is changed.

There is nothing left of

what you used to be.

...he becomes a new person altogether - the

past is finished and gone, everything has

become fresh and new.

2 Corinthians 5:17, Phil.

11

REVELATION KNOWLEDGE

There are two kinds of knowledge: sense knowledge and revelation knowledge. Sense knowledge refers to what you learn through your five senses. Revelation knowledge comes from the Word of God by the Holy Spirit.

An example of revelation knowledge is found in Matthew 16:13-17. Jesus asked His disciples, "Whom do men say that I the Son of man am?" The disciples responded, "Some say that thou art John the Baptist: some, Elias; and others, Jeromias, or one of the prophets." Then Jesus asked, "But whom say ye that I am?" Simon Peter, through revelation knowledge, spoke up, "Thou art the Christ, the Son of the living God." Jesus said to Simon Peter, "Flesh and blood hath not revealed it unto thee, but my Father which is in heaven." In other words, Jesus told Peter, "You did not learn this through your five senses; you learned it through revelation knowledge."

That is why Paul prayed in Ephesians 1:17 that God would "give unto you the spirit of wisdom and revelation in the knowledge of him." Paul isn't referring to just learning more about God. He was referring to knowledge revealed by the Holy Spirit.

REVEALED BY THE HOLY SPIRIT

Revelation knowledge comes when the eyes of your spirit are opened up. It is when the Holy Spirit transmits the things of Christ. God is a Spirit, and His truths are revealed through your spirit. The Holy Spirit transmits the things of Christ to you. You see something that no one else in the natural realm sees. You see that God has done something that is not natural. When Jesus died on the cross, He took every man unto Himself. He died our death. If you go by head knowledge - your senses or mental assent - the Word of God will lose its effectiveness and its power.

> If you go by head knowledge...the Word of God will lose its effectiveness and its power.

When Jesus was crucified Paul was nowhere near, yet he said, "Christ took me to the cross with Him, and I died there with Him," Galatians 2:20, Laubach. Where did he get that information? Paul must have gotten it from God Himself. When did he get that information? He must have gotten it when he was out in the wilderness of Arabia during those years when Jesus came and revealed to him what happened in His death and resurrection. That was revelation knowledge or knowledge revealed by the Holy Spirit.

NEW UNDERSTANDING

Revelation knowledge opens the Word up to you. Through revelation knowledge of Galatians 2:20 you understand, "I have a new identity. It is no longer I who live, but Christ lives in me."

> *Yes, I have shared Messiah's crucifixion. I am living indeed, but it is not I that live, it is Messiah whose life is in me....*
> **Galatians 2:20, Arthur S. Way**

> *I consider myself as having died and now enjoying a second existence, which is simply Jesus using my body.*
> **The Distilled Bible**

Do you think Paul was crucified with Christ? He said he was. He is not saying it exclusively as the Apostle Paul, but he is talking about what happened in the death and resurrection of Christ as your substitute. Jesus became your substitute. Everything He did, He did to the credit of your account.

YOUR IDENTITY WITH CHRIST

It is important to understand your identification with Christ in His crucifixion and resurrection because it is at the center of the Gospel. You won't hear a sermon on this in many churches even if you stay there for ten years. They are trying so hard to deal with everybody's personal problems. They are keeping people from having nervous breakdowns, teaching them how to love their wife or husband, how to discipline their kids, how to get their healing, and how to get their needs met.

If you preach on your identity with Christ in many churches, people will look at you like a cow at a new gate. They will say, "You don't understand. I'm trying to make my refrigerator payment, I've got pain in my lower back, and I'm having trouble with my kids. I need new carpet in my house, I'm dealing with emotional problems and stress, and you are talking about identification with Christ. That's not what I need." Yet an understanding of their identity in Christ is exactly what they need!

> The greater your Word intake, the more Christ will be manifested through you.

The level of manifestation of Christ in you is based on your revelation knowledge of the Word and your mixing faith with it. It is also based upon your willingness to yield to the Holy Spirit because the Holy Spirit is the One Who reveals

Christ — that is His job. The greater your Word intake, the more Christ will be manifested through you.

Every day you can declare, "I was crucified with Christ. It is not my old self who lives, but Christ Himself lives in me. The life I live in this body, I live by faith in the Son of God who loved me and gave Himself for me."

God was working

In Christ,

but He was working

ON US.

For we are His workmanship, created

in Christ Jesus unto good works, which

God hath before ordained that we

should walk in them.

Ephesians 2:10, KJV

12

HOW GOD CHANGES
PEOPLE'S IDENTITIES

Paul had such an extreme identity change, he said, "It's not even me living anymore." That's a pretty radical change! People are trying to get God to help them deal with their problems. Yet He is saying, "As my child, since I am living on the inside of you, just let Me deal with your challenges through you."

Someone said, "The power of God hit Saul of Tarsus so hard on the road to Damascus that it knocked the 'S' off the front of his name and replaced it with a 'P' and he became Paul." His name changed, his identity changed, and his nature changed.

Paul was a Pharisee, a very religious man, and he received a strong revelation of Jesus Christ. When he was hit with the light of God, he went blind for three days. During that time, he fasted and prayed.

A WHOLE NEW IDENTITY

I believe the moment you receive Christ you become a new creation in Him. It takes a while to feed on the Word before you say, "I'm not even the same person anymore. I have a whole new identity."

If you committed a crime and the FBI got hold of you and wanted to give you a new identity to protect you, they would change your address, your Social Security number, and all records concerning every bill that you owe. They would totally wipe out your past to protect you.

God wiped out your old identity when you were born again. He wiped out your past. Every account, sin, or claim the devil had on you has been wiped out. Once you are lost in Christ, the devil can't even find you! Hallelujah!

> *For ye are dead, and your life is hid with Christ in God.*
>
> *Colossians 3:3*

The devil can't even find you unless you stick your fleshly head up and say, "Hey, it's me!" Slap your head and get it back down in there, man! You want to talk about my past, my feelings, and my failures? God says, "I don't want to talk about that. You are dead and your life is hid with Christ in Me. Don't stick your head up. You've got a new identity now."

A NEW LIFE IN CHRIST

God made provision for you to be in Christ even before you were saved, but this new identity did not become yours until you exercised faith in Him when you were born again. You became a new creation in Christ the day you were saved, but it won't become a reality to you unless you walk in the light of the Word. You'll have to feed on the Word, get it engrafted on the inside of you, receive revelation knowledge of the Word, and let the Holy Spirit help you to see your new identity — who you are in Christ and what you have in Him.

> *Therefore, if any one is in union with Christ, he is a new being! His old life has passed away; a new life has begun!*
> *2 Corinthians 5:17, 20th C.R.*

FROM CHILDLESS TO FATHER OF MANY

One of the greatest stories ever written on changing one's identity is found in the greatest book ever written — the Bible. It is the story of God appearing to Abram and Sarai. God basically said, "I'm changing your identity and I'm changing your name. You will never be called Abram again. You are Abraham, which means father of many. And Sarai, I'm changing your name to Sarah, which means you are a princess."

117

I believe every time Sarah and Abraham called each other by their new names, they declared who God said they were. Yet, Abraham, "father of many," didn't have any children at this point in his life.

That's how God does business. If He can get you to agree with Him, to agree with revelation knowledge, His Word will not return unto Him void. It will accomplish what He sent it out to do, and it will prosper in the thing whereto He sent it (Isaiah 55:11). In other words, the Word has the power to produce what it says if God can get you to agree with it.

Abraham became the father of many nations as well as the father of your faith. God totally changed his identity. You wouldn't recognize him years later as the man who left Ur of the Chaldees at God's direction.

FROM COUNTRY BOY TO PROPHET

God is in the business of changing identities. One of my favorite stories of how God totally changed someone's identity is with Saul in 1 Samuel 9 and 10. Saul was looking for his father's donkeys when he met Samuel the prophet. Samuel told him, "Go up before me unto the high place; for ye shall eat with me today, and tomorrow I will let thee go, and will tell thee all that is in thine heart," 1 Samuel 9:19. Then the prophet told Saul, "...You will meet a company of prophets...And the Spirit of the Lord will come upon thee, and thou shalt prophesy with them, and shalt be turned into another man," 1 Samuel 10:5,6. The prophet Samuel was saying, "Saul, you are a country boy, but the Holy Ghost will come on you and you are going to be changed into another man." Saul received a totally new identity.

YOUR VALUE IN CHRIST

How did this happen? He didn't go to every self-help and support group in an attempt to get a new identity. He didn't consult a psychologist or call the psychic hotline! If that had been the case, I would have said, "Saul, you are messed up. You are messing with devils and trying everything after the flesh." You can get a whole new identity when you see who God says you are and what God says you have. Your self-esteem will go right through the roof! You will say, "Glory to God! Look what God says I am. Look at the value God has given me in Christ."

The devil wants to destroy your dignity and self-esteem. But when you see your value in what God has done for you in the death and resurrection of Christ, you will hold your head up high and forget those things which are behind. You will say, "The person who did those things, acted that way, and thought that way is dead." Glory to God!

CHANGED FROM WITHIN

God can give you a new identity. He made you, so He ought to be able to remake you. He is the manufacturer! We are not dealing with someone who just repairs. We are talking about the One who creates people. God creates people out of nothing! No scientist has ever figured out how to make people. Natural man can make houses, toasters, and color TV's, but they are not making people! God is the Creator. He is the original people person. He specializes in making people over again and giving them brand new identities.

> *Arise, and go down to the potter's house, and there I will cause thee to hear my words. Then I went down to the potter's house, and, behold, he wrought a work on the wheels. And the vessel that he made of clay was marred in the hand of the potter: so he made it again another vessel, as seemed good to the potter to make it.*
> *Jeremiah 18:2-4*

God was telling Jeremiah, "You go down to the potter's house, and I am going to show you that when people have defects in them, I will make them over again." God is in the business of changing people's identities. He does it from the inside out. When you are born again, your spirit is recreated. Then He builds from the inside out — changing your mind, renewing it, rebuilding your thinking and attitudes, and then changing your body and your actions.

> **For it is God which worketh in you both to will and to do of his good pleasure.**
>
> **Philippians 2:13**

FROM COWARD TO MIGHTY MAN OF VALOR

Another classic, yet radical identity change that took place in the Bible was with Gideon. He was living in a hole in the ground and hiding out from the enemy. If you live in a hole in the ground long enough, you will develop a certain philosophy about life. If you don't think so, go find someone who lives under a bridge. If you talk to them for very long, you will find out they don't just have a bridge externally; they have a bridge internally in their thinking and attitude.

When Jesus came to preach the Gospel to the poor, He didn't just pass out a bunch of fish sandwiches!

When Jesus came to preach the Gospel to the poor, He didn't just pass out a bunch of fish sandwiches! He taught them the ways and thoughts of God. He taught them that they didn't have to be poor or sick or defeated anymore. Jesus is still changing people's identities!

Every time Gideon tried to do anything, the Midianites destroyed it. In the midst of his hole-in-the-ground existence, God sent an angel to Gideon with a message, "The Lord is with thee, thou mighty man of valour," Judges 6:12. God has a sense of humor because at this time in Gideon's life, there was no evidence of valor! Yet, God's Word is all that is needed.

> *...he quickeneth the dead, and calleth those things which be not as though they were.*
>
> *Romans 4:17*

God's Word will cause *nothing* to become *something*. Gideon chewed on God's Word to him — you mighty man of valour — until he finally swallowed it. Then with trumpets, pitchers, lamps, and a cry of the sword of the Lord, Gideon and his three hundred man army whipped the enemy (Judges 7:20-22). Any time you get involved with God and His Word, He will totally change the way you see yourself and the way you see life. The Word of God changes everything.

MY NAME IS ROCK

When Simon Peter received revelation knowledge of who Jesus was — the Christ, the Son of the living God (Matthew 16:16) — Jesus turned to him and said, "I'm telling you who you are, Simon. No longer will you be tossed to and fro. I am changing your name to Rock."

Can't you just see Simon responding to the people who wouldn't accept his new name? You know, "Your mama named you Simon." Peter totally identified with who Jesus said he was: "Jesus is the One who named me, and my name is rock!" Jesus changed Peter's identity.

LET ME TELL YOU WHO I AM

It is important to understand who you are in Christ because the devil knows if you know your identity. In Acts 19, the seven sons of Sceva, without having a relationship with Jesus (which would give them authority to use His name), tried to use the name of Jesus to cast out evil spirits. An evil spirit said to them, "Jesus I know, and Paul I know; but who are you?" Because they didn't know their identity in Christ, the scripture says, "The evil spirit...leaped on them, and overcame them, and prevailed against them, so that they fled out of that house naked and wounded," Acts 19:16.

YOUR IDENTITY IN THE WORD

As a born-again, Spirit-filled teenager, I struggled with my own identity. While in my bedroom studying where Jesus went into the synagogue to preach His first sermon in Luke 4, I read, "And there was delivered unto Him the book of the prophet Esaias. And when He had opened the book, He found the place where it was written," Luke 4:17.

The Holy Ghost spoke to me, "Though Jesus was deity, He laid aside His deity power when He became a man, and in His humanity, He had to study the Word to find out who He was." I believe when Jesus was ten, eleven, or twelve years old, He found out who He was by reading it in the scriptures. Jesus identified with the Word as He read Isaiah 61:1, "The Spirit of the Lord God is upon me; because the Lord hath anointed me to preach good tidings unto the meek; he hath sent me to bind up the brokenhearted, to proclaim liberty to the captives, and the opening of the prison to them that are bound."

> *And Jesus increased in wisdom and stature, and*
> *in favour with God and man.*
>
> *Luke 2:52*

You will find your identity in the same book — the Bible. You won't find it in some psychology book or by trying to mimic a movie star. Many people, not just teenagers, have an identity crisis. They comb their hair like someone they see on TV. They watch some cowboy movie and think they are John Wayne, or they see a motorcycle rider and think they need a motorcycle and a bandanna around their head too.

The devil will do everything he can to steal the Word from you to keep you from understanding your new identity in Christ. He wants you to see yourself in the natural. He will even get you to study your family tree which never produced anything but a bunch of nuts!

In identifying with your family instead of with Christ, you may say, "The reason I am divorced is because my mother, grandmother, and great grandmother were divorced. My daddy was an alcoholic, my grandpa was an alcoholic, so I'm an alcoholic. It just runs in my family." You need to find your identity from God. He knows who you are. You are an individual created to reflect His glory. If the devil can get you to flip-flop mentally with your reasoning and your flesh, he will totally defeat you.

CHRIST LIVES IN YOU

The Apostle Paul said, "I only have one identity and that is who I am in Christ Jesus. I don't identify with anything or anyone else. I was crucified with Christ, nevertheless I live; yet not I, but Christ lives in me."

You can go to almost any insane asylum and find

someone who thinks he is Napoleon. Often people are controlled by familiar spirits and natural connections instead of taking the Word of God and letting God establish their identity. Jesus initiated your identification with God when He became a man.

In His humanity, Jesus identified with you so He could know how you feel, what you go through, and the struggles you face. He didn't totally identify with you though, until He went to the cross where He took your sinful condition and your curse. Jesus sealed man's identification with God on the cross because when Jesus died on the cross, He was not a man for one human

> Never again will you identify with defeat, failure, depression, fear, sickness, poverty, or lack once your identification with Christ is sealed.

generation. He became a man forever. He is still a man right now, seated at the right hand of God representing a new, victorious humanity.

Once you understand your identification with Christ in His death, burial, and resurrection, it will take you from His death, burial, and resurrection right through to triumph where Christ is seated at the right hand of God. Never again will you identify with defeat, failure, depression, fear, sickness, poverty, or lack once your identification with Christ is sealed. Why? Because it is no longer you who live, but Christ lives in you!

Some people may never know their earthly father. However, they don't have to spend their entire life with a big gap in their souls. They can just say, "I am identified with Christ and God is my Father." That means no longer are you going under, but you are going over. I was under when I had no identification with Christ, but God stamped in my spirit the death, burial, and resurrection of Christ.

You are a totally different person than when you were born. Even if your daddy or mama was a failure, when you are born again, you are re-fathered! If you come from a dysfunctional family, when you are born again you receive a functional family — the family of God. That's your identification with Christ.

CONFESS YOUR IDENTITY IN CHRIST

Don't you ever let the devil bring up your past, show you pictures of it, and say, "That's who you are." You tell him, "You are a lying dog. Get out of my life. That old person is dead and gone. I am crucified with Christ; nevertheless I live — Christ Himself lives in me." Begin to confess what God's Word says about your identification with Christ.

In Christ, the world is crucified unto me and I unto the world (Galatians 6:14). Since I am risen with Christ, I seek those things which are above. My affection is set on things above, not on things on the earth. My life is hid with Christ in God (Colossians 3:1-3). I am buried with Christ by baptism into death. Just as Christ was raised up from the dead by the glory of the Father, even so I walk in newness of life (Romans 6:4). My old sin nature is crucified with Christ. I no longer serve sin (Romans 6:6). God, who is rich in mercy and love for me, has quickened me together with Christ, raised me up, and made me sit together in heavenly places in Christ Jesus (Ephesians 2:4-6).

Now that we have established a foundation of who you are in Christ, in the next chapter we will look at the inheritance He left for you that is yours now!

Notes:

God has made us

100% righteous In Christ.

You cannot be 25, 50, 75,

or 90% righteous - In Christ

you have been made

100% righteous.

For in Him dwelleth all the fullness

of the Godhead bodily. And ye are

complete in Him which is the head of all

principality and power.

Colossians 2:9-10, KJV

13

YOUR INHERITANCE IN CHRIST

Therefore if any man be in Christ, he is a new creature [or creation]; old things are passed away; behold, all things are become new. And all things are of God, who hath reconciled us to himself by Jesus Christ, and hath given to us the ministry of reconciliation.

2 Corinthians 5:17-18

When Paul says "and all things are of God" in verse 18, he is not just saying that everything is of God. He is literally talking about all of these things of the new creation. Other translations say, "This is the work of God." The Apostle Paul is talking about *who you are* in Christ Jesus. He is talking about the miracle of the new birth — what happens when you are born again.

131

IN CHRIST-ED

Several scriptures use this phrase *in Christ*. When I was seventeen years old it really helped me to look up all the in Christ scriptures — all 130 of them. When you are born again, I like to say, "You are in Christ-ed!" As a believer in Jesus Christ, you are in Christ, and whatever is true of someone in Christ is true of you.

As I went through the in Christ scriptures as a teenager, I would get my guitar and sing and pray them over and over again. I would declare, "I am who God says I am, and I have what God says I have. I can do what God says I can do." I did that for hours. I'm not talking about just during a youth revival or camp meeting; I'm talking about day after day. I sang and prayed the Ephesians prayers everyday.

That the God of our Lord Jesus Christ, the Father of glory, may give unto you the spirit of wisdom and revelation in the knowledge of Him; that the eyes of your understanding would be enlightened; that you would know the hope of His calling; the riches of His inheritance in the saints; the exceeding greatness of His power to us who believe, according to the working of

*His mighty power, which He wrought in Christ
when He raised Him from the dead.*
Ephesians 1:17-20

If you will pray these prayers every day, I guarantee your life will be different in six months. If you are happy with your life the way it is, just keep doing what you are doing, and it will stay that way or even get worse. If you want things to change for the better, I challenge you to pray the Ephesians prayers every day. Pray them over your children, even if they are grown and married. Pray them over your husband or wife.

Something happened in God's economy when He raised Christ from the dead:

- Righteousness was restored to man
- The devil was defeated
- The curse was broken
- Man was restored to fellowship with God
  Redemption was accomplished

These provisions became yours when you said, "Yes, Jesus, I surrender to You. I want You to be Lord of my life." Once you said "yes" to Jesus, you were in Christ-ed! All that God did in Christ became personally yours.

To be in Christ means that you have been blessed with all spiritual blessings in heavenly places in Christ (Ephesians

1:3). As a teenager, I would sing, "I am God's workmanship, created in Christ Jesus for good works, which God ordained that I should walk in," Ephesians 2:10. God doesn't make trash, you know. If you are the workmanship of God, you must be something wonderful!

GOD HAS PREPARED THE WAY

God has prepared a path ahead of time for His children. When you walk in that path, everything you need is found on it.

> The moment you confess Jesus Christ as your Lord and Savior, your spirit receives eternal life.

When you are born again, you pass from death to life. This is referring to spiritual death. The moment you confess Jesus Christ as your Lord and Savior, your spirit receives eternal life.

> *And you hath he quickened, who were dead in trespasses and sins.*
>
> *Ephesians 2:1*

Did you know that you can get saved in your car, working in your backyard, or walking down the aisle in the grocery store? Even a person who cries out to Jesus with his or her last breath of life is born again.

> *For whosoever shall call upon the name of the*
> *Lord shall be saved.*
>
> *Romans 10:13*

Before you received Jesus, you weren't *physically* or *mentally* dead, but you were *spiritually* dead, which means you were alienated or separated from God. Because you were spiritually dead, Satan was able to exercise dominion over you.

FREED FROM SATAN'S DOMINION

The moment you were born again, your spirit received eternal life. You left Satan's dominion and entered the dominion of the Lord Jesus Christ. Legally, Satan no longer has any control over you. In fact, he cannot touch you. You are in Christ. You are in this world, but you are not of it. Satan will still try to come against you, but you have left his jurisdiction.

> *Who hath delivered us from the power of*
> *darkness, and hath translated us into the*
> *kingdom of His dear Son.*
>
> *Colossians 1:13*

> *...the authority of the darkness.*
>
> *Rotherham's*

To explain leaving Satan's authority or jurisdiction, think

of a policeman assigned to Alexandria, Louisiana. He has no jurisdiction in Texas, so he can't give you a ticket in Texas. He has no authority there. The moment you pass from death to life, you leave Satan's jurisdiction and enter into the jurisdiction of the Lord Jesus Christ. So you can say, "Mr. Devil, you have no dominion over me. Sickness, poverty, and sin, you have no dominion over me because I left death and have entered life."

> *Verily, verily, I say unto you, he that heareth My word, and believeth on Him that sent me, hath everlasting life, and shall not come into condemnation; but is passed from death unto life.*
>
> *John 5:24*
>
> *...has spiritual life...has transferred from the death region to the life region.*
>
> *Jordan's*

There are 130 things that are true about you right now. You are the righteousness of God in Christ. You are always triumphant in Christ. Victory is yours. Christ has redeemed you. Redemption is yours in Christ. If the devil cannot stop you from getting saved, then after you are saved he wants to cheat you out of your inheritance and keep you ignorant of what belongs to you in Christ.

For in him dwelleth all the fullness of the godhead bodily. And ye are complete in him, which is the head of all principality and power.

Colossians 2:9,10

That simply means the moment you are born again, you get in Christ-ed and whatever is in Christ is now in you. When you are born again your spirit is joined to Jesus.

JOINED TO CHRIST

But he that is joined unto the Lord is one spirit.

1 Corinthians 6:17

But he that is in union with the Master is one with Him in spirit.

Weymouth's

But if you give yourself to the Lord, you and Christ are joined together as one person.

The Living Bible

If the only purpose for salvation was for you to go to heaven, God would have built in a special death mechanism that as soon as you confess Jesus as Lord, you would die right then. Actually, God saved you so heaven could get on the inside of you, and then you could change the world around you.

God saved you so you could bring heaven into this earth and change the world. God saved you to change your children, your neighborhood, and your city.

> God saved you so heaven could get on the inside of you, and then you could change the world around you.

God saved you so He could move on the inside of you. He saved you so your mind would work right. He saved you so you wouldn't be a victim of sin, bad habits, lust, and deception. He freed you from Satan's dominion so when you die, you won't wonder why you lived. God saved you for Christ to be formed in you! Instead of sitting around with a sanctimonious look on your face like you've been sucking oats through a gas pipe, what would happen if you found out what really took place when you were saved?

DELIVERED FROM SIN

The word "saved" means daily delivered from sin's dominion (Romans 5:10, Amplified). It means delivered not only from sin that grips and controls people's lives, but from the effects of sin that shut down the glory of God and your production as a child of God. When sin takes hold of you, you are absolutely worthless to the Kingdom of God. Your confidence goes, the gift of God in you gets messed up, and you sit around in deception, shame, and guilt trying to smile and act like everything is all right.

In Acts 9, we see the story of the Apostle Paul's conversion. He was a Pharisee who had studied and knew the scriptures well. Yet, he realized that his dead religion could not compare to what happened to him on the road to Damascus when he met Jesus.

> God saved you to conform you to the image of His Son

Paul immediately said to the Lord, "Who are you Lord? What will you have me to do?" Acts 9:5,6. The moment you become a new creation, you need to say, "Jesus, I want to know you and I want to know what you want me to do."

When you were saved, Jesus moved on the inside of you so He could invade your mind, your soul, your emotions, your intellect, and your body. He filled you up with His life so it can flow out of you into your husband or wife and your children.

God saved you to conform you to the image of His Son so you could be all God has created and designed you to be. There's more to life than thirty years of mortgage payments, polyester suits, Toyotas, Cadillacs, and Mercedes! When you are saved, you are put in union with Christ so the same life, glory, joy, authority, power, inheritance, future, blessings — the same stuff that is in Christ comes in you!

A SPIRITUAL CONNECTION

Some translators refer to the in Christ phrase as "in union with Christ." When your spirit is joined to Christ, that means the unseen part of you on the inside is connected to Christ. You say, "How could that be?" It's not like you have a telephone line that goes from your spirit through the roof up into the heavens. Obviously, airplanes would get tangled up in it! If a network is broadcasting out of New York City, you can tune in with a TV set and a receiver and receive the exact program at the same time. Even if you are living in the woods some 2,000 miles away, wearing your boots, driving your four-wheeler, and piping in the sunshine, still there is an *unseen connection* between your TV set and what is going on in New York City.

The moment you are born again, God gives your spirit a receiver and He tunes it in to heaven. The same thing that is playing in heaven booms on the inside of you! Though you used to be cursed and bound, confused and messed up, you can tune in to a new picture! You are in union with Christ. Now you can see a picture of *all* that God wants you to be — a picture of the redeeming power of Jesus Christ, a picture of what God has planned for you to be. Hallelujah!

> The moment you are born again, God gives your spirit a receiver and He tunes it in to heaven.

TO BE LIKE JESUS

When God made you a new creation in Christ, He didn't make you to be defeated, confused, sick, poor, beat up, and to live on barely-get-along street. He made you to be a conqueror! Some people say, "Brother, you preach all that healing and prosperity stuff and it just makes me sick because I don't need it. I just want to be like Jesus." Well, that's honorable of you. Did you know that Jesus isn't sick? He isn't poor either.

Do you think He is sitting on the throne saying, "Oh, my stomach is hurting. I don't know how I'm going to make it. I've got some payments coming up at the end of this month. I've been talking to the Father about them, but I don't know if I'm going to make it. I am so tired!" That's not the way Jesus is. He is seated at the right hand of God, and the Bible says His enemies are way beneath His feet. All power in heaven and in earth has been given to Him. Everything the Father has is His.

> *I am He that liveth, and was dead; and, behold, I am alive forevermore, Amen; and have the keys of hell and of death.*
> *Revelation 1:18*

Jesus is not sitting up there barely getting along. He is saying to every born-again believer, "I've got all power in heaven and earth. If you need it, you can get it from Me. If I don't have it in stock, I will make it just for you!"

MORE LIKE JESUS

You can be more like Jesus. He healed the sick and cast out devils. When Jesus came into a town, things changed. The devil is faithful to come back and visit. He will come back and say, "If you are really saved...." Some people have never decided if they are saved or not. From the preaching they are hearing, it is probably a wonder they have even hung around!

The preacher says, "I know you did everything the Book says, but you can't ever tell." What do you mean, "You can't ever tell"? If God said it and you did it, you are saved. You can say, "You can't ever tell" all the way to your funeral. You can keep all the rules, quit wearing earrings, get all the make-up off your face, get baptized three different ways, speak in tongues, shake all over, and still not know if you are saved.

Being in Christ has nothing to do with your feelings. It has everything to do with the Word of God and the integrity of God's Word. It has everything to do with what Jesus did for you 2,000 years ago. You can get up every morning and say, "I am a new creation in Christ Jesus. Old things are passed away, and everything has become new."

Some people are still talking about what happened to them when they were ten years old. There is not a thing in the world a psychologist or anyone else can do for you if something messed your life up when you were ten. Jesus can do something!

In Him you can become brand new. Old things are passed away. There is a department of your being — your spirit — where at the moment you are born again, old things are passed away and everything becomes new.

There is not one little molecule left of what you used to be — not a trace! You can get all the specialists you want to try to find a trace of what you used to be, but they won't find it. They can never dig it up. It is gone forever. God will never speak of it because it doesn't exist anymore. That's good news, and it will set you free.

God made you a

new creature

In Christ, but

you must put on

the new man.

And that ye put on the new man, which after God is

created in righteousness and true holiness.

Ephesians 4:24, KJV

...put on the new person that you are.

Adams

Clothe yourselves with that new and better self,

which has been created to resemble God in the

righteousness and holiness which

come from the truth.

Weym.

14

THE UNSEEN CONNECTION

The Holy Spirit is the Spirit of truth. If you would listen to Him, He would keep you out of a lot of trouble — trouble in business, in relationships, and in church. You have a partner to walk out your new life with in Christ. His name is the Holy Spirit or the Holy Ghost. "Howbeit when He, the Spirit of truth is come...," John 16:13.

In this scripture, Jesus describes the work of the Holy Ghost. If the preacher isn't telling you the truth, the Holy Spirit will say, "That isn't true." But if you have the Holy Ghost on the inside of you and the preacher is telling the truth, He will say, "That is the truth."

You may be thinking, "Truth doesn't excite me." What does? The casinos? Do you like all the lights and the truth that is spoken there? They will call you everything you want to be called. "Mr. Wonderful, you might be a millionaire tonight."

But remember, they didn't build that place with winners! They are even glad when you win because you will stick around and lose another $5,000. Then you will go to church and not even pay your tithes. You need a slap on the head!

What does the Holy Spirit, the Spirit of truth, do? "He will guide you into all truth," John 16:13. As you read your Bible, you need to invite your Holy Spirit partner by saying, "Holy Spirit, let's read the Bible. Help me and guide me into all truth. Show me something, Holy Spirit." Since the Holy Spirit wrote it, He ought to know what it means!

YOUR HELPER

The Holy Spirit will keep you from just reading the Word with your head. He wants to show you the Bible in the light of redemption. He will show you the weightier matters and things that are of first importance. The Holy Spirit will help you read your Bible. He will show you the things that are the most important. He won't take something out of context and mess your head up with it. That is the devil's role. The devil can quote the Bible and get you all messed up. But the Holy Spirit will show you the whole picture. He will show you who you are and what you have in Christ.

Smith Wigglesworth said, "The Holy Spirit never brings condemnation. He always reveals the blood of Jesus. He always lifts and helps." He tells you the truth to help you because if you keep going the way you are going, you will get messed up!

Thank God for the Holy Ghost! Have you ever heard someone say, "I don't need to listen to the Holy Ghost?" Your wife is not your Holy Ghost and neither is your husband. Every person can have a relationship with the Holy Spirit. The moment you are born again, you pass from death to life and the Spirit of God comes to live on the inside of you. Your body becomes the temple of the Holy Spirit.

> Every person can have a relationship with the Holy Spirit.

REVEAL THINGS TO COME

...For he shall not speak of himself; but whatsoever he shall hear, that shall he speak...
John 16:13

What does it mean, "Whatsoever he shall hear, that shall he speak"? Who does the Holy Spirit hang out with? He hangs out with the Father and the Son, so whatever He hears them say is what He says. Verse 13 concludes, "...and he will shew you things to come."

If you want to know what is happening, you do not have to call the psychic network and ask, "What do you see in my future?" I see you going broke if you stay on that line very long! Four dollars a minute, yet you come to church and put in a dollar. You need another slap! Four dollars a minute talking to a lying devil. If it's not a devil, it's a fool who looks under cards. The cards are arranged according to states. In Louisiana, for example, they put hunting and fishing on the card. When someone from Louisiana calls they say, "I see squirrel hunting in your future. I see a swamp in your future. I see an alligator in your future. I see crawdads in your future." That's ridiculous!

If you hang out with the Holy Ghost and become sensitive to Him, He will show you things to come about your life, your future, your children, your marriage, and your business. He will show you things to come about where you are going to live in the future, but He can't talk to you if you don't listen.

Be still and get with the Holy Ghost — talk to Him. Worship God and worship Jesus, then say, "Holy Spirit, help me read the Word. Show me things to come. I don't want to miss the will of God for my life. Help me."

The Holy Spirit showed me the house we are living in right now a year before we moved into it. As soon as Trina and I saw it I said, "That's our house. I don't know how much it costs, but I know it's ours." Before my son, Aaron, was born, I got up in the church where I was youth pastor and said, "My first child will be a boy. The Holy Ghost told me that it is a son." Then I said, "Don't bring any girl's clothes because it's a boy."

Some people said, "We don't want you to be

disappointed." I didn't go by a sonogram because Trina didn't have one — I went by the Holy Ghost. One lady brought me a little dress for Aaron. I said, "My boy ain't wearing no dress! You just take it back and exchange it." She got mad and said, "You're just hardheaded, aren't you?" I said, "No, I have been praying every night for an hour and a half, and the Holy Ghost told me the baby is a boy." In the fullness of time my son, Aaron, was born.

Two years later when Trina was pregnant again, I prayed and the Holy Ghost said, "This one is a girl." I got up in the pulpit where I was pastoring and said, "This baby is a girl. Don't bring any boy's clothes." Again, I went by what the Holy Ghost told me because Trina didn't have a sonogram. I had a Holy Ghost picture. He told me it was a girl. In the fullness of time my daughter, Alicia, was born.

INSIDE INFORMATION

If you will spend time with the Holy Ghost, you will learn to hear His voice and He will tell you what is going to happen a year from now, three years from now, or five years from now. He will tell you what is going to happen so you can get ready for it. The Holy Ghost can show you tragedy that is about to come in your life, in your children's lives, or in someone else's life if there isn't a change. He will show you this not to produce fear, but so you can change it in prayer. This is one of the new creation benefits. With the Holy Spirit inside of you, you will have inside information!

> *Howbeit when he, the Spirit of truth, is come, he will guide you into all truth: for he shall not speak of himself; but whatsoever he shall hear, that shall he speak: and he will shew you things to come...He shall glorify me: for he shall receive of mine, and shall shew it unto you.*
>
> *John 16:13,14*

GLORIFIES JESUS

This means when you are full of the Holy Spirit, He will glorify Jesus. If things are happening in your life that are not bringing glory to Jesus, you can change them by praying in the Holy Ghost. He wants everyone to see what Jesus has done for them.

> *...he shall receive of mine, and shall shew it unto you.*
>
> *All things that the Father hath are mine; therefore said I, that he shall take of mine, and shall shew it unto you.*
>
> *John 16:14-15*

JESUS ON THE INSIDE

The Holy Spirit is your "unseen connection" between heaven and earth. You are in union with Christ by virtue of the Spirit of God, so that whatever is playing in heaven is playing in your spirit. You don't have the same capacity as heaven, but you have the same quality. You don't have the same capacity as God, but you do have the same quality of life that God has. You can enjoy a quality of life that doesn't come from the Republicans, Democrats, welfare, or social programs. You can enjoy a quality of life that no company can guarantee you, with no special help when you retire. You can say, "It is good because I have the same life in me that is in God right now."

On a recent "700 Club" program, Ben Kinchlow interviewed an african american man who said, "I was raised in the ghetto, but the ghetto never got inside of me. There were drugs all around me, but no drugs ever got in me. Violence and crime were all around me, but they never got in me. Disaster was all around me, but it never got in me. I am here because of Jesus who got inside of me!" Too many people let their environment shape and control them but this man said, "Greater is he [Jesus Christ] that is in me, than he [the devil] that is in the world," 1 John 4:4.

You don't have to adjust your TV set according to the filth, sin, lust, and violence that are all around you. You can adjust your set to what is playing in heaven: holiness, fire, purity, love, righteousness, glory. I've got my set hooked up to heaven. How? I've got an unseen connection — the Holy Ghost. I am adjusting my set right now. It is tuned in. Where does all this happen? It happens in your spirit once you are born again.

SPIRIT, SOUL, AND BODY

You say, "If that is so, why am I having so many problems? It just doesn't seem real to me." You are made up of three parts; spirit, soul, and body. Even after you are saved, something still has to happen in your soul — your mind, will, and emotions. Otherwise, even though you are a new creature in Christ, you are still acting like the world and your spirit is held hostage to an unrenewed mind, feelings, and emotions. All kinds of trash from your past, everybody's opinions, and this world are shaping you. Your spirit is literally held hostage until your mind is renewed with the daily washing of God's Word.

FEED ON THE WORD

You will never be what God intends for you to be until your mind, will, and emotions are dominated by God's Word. When you feed your spirit on the Word and allow the Holy Spirit to work in you, your mind will be renewed. The same power that is working in your spirit will move up into your head. Then God will start dealing with some of your habits and attitudes.

Initially some people respond, "I'm not changing, I don't care what the Bible says. God understands that this is the way I am. I like a little sin on weekends and R-rated movies and pornography every now and then. I like to tell lies and dirty jokes. Sometimes I lose my temper, but that's just the way I am. I'll tithe when I want to. I'm not changing." The Holy Spirit has a rocket missile launcher going from your spirit to your head. It is launched as you feed upon God's Word.

John the Baptist said, "When Jesus comes, He is going to take an axe and cut the roots of that tree." If you will be still long enough in the presence of God and say, "Okay, Jesus, go ahead. I am a new creation in Christ. I refuse to be bound by habits, attitudes, sins, or ideas that have controlled my soul, my family, and my life for ten or twenty years. I refuse to be bound. Go ahead Jesus, let's have some changes around here." Then Jesus will start cleaning house!

> *...Put off concerning the former conversation [lifestyle] the old man, which is corrupt according to deceitful lusts; And be renewed in the spirit of your mind; And that ye put on the new man, which after God is created in righteousness and true holiness.*
>
> *Ephesians 4:22-24*

BECOMING LIKE CHRIST

Even though you are born again and a new creature in Christ, it is a decision you must make to say, "Okay, Holy Ghost, lead me into all truth." The Holy Spirit will tell you the truth and the truth will set you free. Why? So you can be all that God wants you to be. Wrong attitudes, compromise, sin, and disobedience will stop the flow of the life of God so the image of Christ is not working in you and cannot be fully formed in you. You will end up dying and wonder why you ever lived.

Once you find out who you are in Christ and let Him be formed in you, every gift, talent, calling, and purpose of God will begin to take shape in your life. God not only meets your needs and gives you bonuses and benefits, but as someone said, "The greatest reward for obeying God is not what you get; it's what you become!"

Sometimes you don't know what the true personality of a person is like because of all the things that have happened and all the trash piled on top of him or her. Let the Holy Spirit begin to work in your spirit, lead you into all truth, and show you who you are in Christ. Let that same picture coming from heaven play in you. You will begin to say, "I am who God says I am. I have what God says I have. I can do what

> The greatest reward for obeying God is not what you get; it's what you become!

God says I can do. Christ has redeemed me."

It's time for change — I'm not talking about moving to another house. I'm talking about a move on the inside of you. Make the decision and pray, "Lord, change me!"

You are such a
different person in Christ
you will have to let
God introduce you
to your new self.

When someone becomes a
Christian, he becomes a brand
new person inside.
He is not the same any
more. A new life has begun.
2 Corinthians 5:17, TLB

15

ACKNOWLEDGING EVERY GOOD THING THAT IS IN YOU IN CHRIST

That the communication of thy faith may become effectual by the acknowledging of every good thing which is in you in Christ Jesus.

Philemon 6

[And I pray] that the participation in and sharing of your faith may produce and promote full recognition and appreciation and understanding and precise knowledge of every good [thing] that is ours in [our identification with] Christ Jesus [and unto His glory].

Amplified

When you are born again, you are in Christ. Another way to say it is, "You look a whole lot better in Christ than you do outside of Him!" There are a lot of good things that you can

157

acknowledge when you are in Christ. You can acknowledge who you are and what you have in Him. Paul is not talking about

You look a whole lot better in Christ than you do outside of Him!

everything that is going to be yours, he is talking about every good thing that is yours now in your identification with Christ.

EVERY GOOD THING IN CHRIST

Often we spend too much time focusing on our bad qualities and what is wrong with us. If you look at what is wrong with you long enough, it will get worse. Paul is saying that for our faith to become effective or effectual, we need to acknowledge every good thing that is ours in Christ. Your faith won't work unless you acknowledge some things. How do you acknowledge them? By confessing, speaking, or acting on the Word of God.

When Paul says, "every good thing," he must mean that there is more than one good thing in you because you are in Christ. You can't acknowledge every good thing that is yours in Christ if you don't know every good thing that is yours in Him. Once you know some good things that are yours in Christ, your faith still won't work unless you acknowledge these things. Every believer needs to have a daily acknowledgement or confession of who he or she is and what he or she has in Christ.

You may question, "How long do I need to do this?" For

the rest of your life! If you want your faith to work for you, you must continue to acknowledge every good thing that is yours in Christ. When you first get up in the morning and look at yourself in the mirror, or before you eat breakfast, you can take time to pray and acknowledge some of the good things of who you are in Christ.

When you are driving your truck or car, while you are sitting at a traffic light, instead of doing something unprofitable or listening to some foolishness on the radio, begin to confess who you are and what you have in Christ. It will change your prayer life because often you will quit asking God for things that the Word says already belong to you! The terms in Christ, in Him, or in Whom refer to who you are in union with Christ. There are certain things that are yours simply because you are in union with Him. Wisdom, righteousness, sanctification, and redemption are yours because you are in Christ.

> If you want your faith to work for you, you must continue to acknowledge every good thing that is yours in Christ.

> *But of him [of God] are ye in Christ Jesus, who of God is made unto us wisdom, and righteousness, and sanctification, and redemption.*
>
> *1 Corinthians 1:30*

GOD'S WAY OF THINKING

Wisdom is God's way of thinking. God doesn't necessarily think the way you do, and He doesn't always see things the way you see them. If you want to see yourself the way God sees you, get the Word out and see what He says about you. Wisdom has to do with the revelation of all that God has done for you in the death, burial, and resurrection of Christ.

To make wisdom effective in your life, you must acknowledge it. Before you go to bed at night, you need to say, "I thank God that I am in Christ Jesus and He is made unto me wisdom. I don't have to go through life with my own thinking, my own plans, my own ways, or my own ideas. I have God's thoughts, His ways, His plans, and His ideas. Jesus is made unto me wisdom."

RIGHT STANDING WITH GOD

Jesus is made unto you righteousness, which is right standing with God. Once you are born again, you have the same standing with God that Jesus has. Hallelujah!

DEDICATION TO GOD

Jesus is made unto you sanctification, which is separation from the world and dedication to God. What Jesus has begun in your life, He will bring to full completion. He is the author and the finisher of your faith.

DELIVERANCE AND FREEDOM

Jesus is made unto you redemption, which means deliverance or freedom through the payment of a price. Jesus paid the price for your freedom and deliverance in every area of your life —healing for your body, joy, freedom from oppression and depression, and freedom from poverty and the curse.

Jesus is made unto you wisdom, righteousness, sanctification, and redemption. Every day you can say, "Jesus is made unto me wisdom, righteousness, sanctification, and redemption. I am in Him." You may be thinking, "I know all that is in the Bible, but it doesn't seem real to me." It will become real to you when you begin to acknowledge every good thing that is yours in Christ.

THE WORKMANSHIP OF GOD

"Therefore if any man be in Christ, he is a new creature: old things are passed away; behold, all things are become new," 2 Corinthians 5:17. Verse 18 begins, "And all things are of God...," which means this is the work of God. Paul is saying that the moment you were born again, you are in Christ, and you are a new creature. Old things are passed away and everything has become new.

> *...the old condition has passed away, a new condition has come.*
>
> **2 Corinthians 5:17, Williams**

The old condition from which you have been redeemed is the curse of the law, which includes poverty, sickness, confusion, fear, sin, and the devil's domination of your life. When does the "old condition" pass away and the "new condition" come? It doesn't happen over a process of ten or twenty years. It happens the moment you are born again because of the grace of God. The moment you are saved, you become a new creation in Christ.

God would not make an unrighteous new creature because He already had an unrighteous old creature!

One way to say it is, "God would not make an unrighteous new creature because He already had an unrighteous old creature!" Why would He make an unrighteous new creature? This means that if you are a new creature in Christ, you are the righteousness of God in Christ (2 Corinthians 5:21).

THE REALM OF GOD

Do you think God is going to make trash? He is not going to make a confused new creature, a bound new creature, or a defeated new creature. This means the moment you are born again, He puts all of the ingredients in you that are necessary for you to be victorious in life.

When my wife Trina and I went on a cruise, we went scuba diving with the masks, special breathing equipment, and flippers on our feet. Underwater we saw some of the most beautiful fish we have ever seen in our lives. It is a whole new world that you can't see from ground level. Likewise, the moment you are born again, a whole new world opens up to you.

Jesus said, "...except a man be born again, he cannot see the kingdom of God," John 3:3. This means the minute you are born again, you can see the things you couldn't see before. You can see into the realm of God. You can see the power of God. You can see all that God has done for you in Christ. You move into a whole new dimension the moment you are born again!

You can scuba dive in these scripture realities and look for a while, or you can go ahead and get one of those tanks, put it on your back, and submerge for thirty minutes or an hour. You might ask, "How in the world do you submerge?" When God's Spirit is moving and you get in God's presence, He will take you underwater and submerge you in Christ! He will identify you with Christ and show you who you are in Him.

This is not something you try to be; it is who you are. It is not something you try to produce. It is something God has produced for you. You are not trying to make it so. God made it so, and you can declare, "It is so."

LAUGH AT THE DEVIL

Years ago I heard about a young man who was in a Teen Challenge program after blowing his mind on drugs. After taking a hundred hits of LSD at one time, he lost his mind. He sat on the front row in chapel day after day after day, totally out of it. One day he snapped to, stomped his foot, and started laughing.

He was asked, "What happened?" This young man said, "2 Corinthians 5:17 hit me. As soon as it hit me, I started laughing." From that day, he walked around the Teen Challenge Center every day saying, "I am a new creature in Christ. Ha-ha-ha on the devil." He had been like a vegetable, but the Word of God is powerful. It doesn't matter what damage the devil has done in your life. If you will sit under the Word and feed on the Word, it is full of life and power.

God restored his mind and he went into the ministry. Without the input of God's Word, he wouldn't have amounted to anything. But the Word revealed to him his identification with Christ. He started acknowledging it! He acknowledged it by daily confessing, "I am a new creature in Christ. Ha-ha-ha on the devil." He did that day after day. People in mental institutions could have their minds restored by hearing the Word of God over and over again because the Word works.

YOURS RIGHT NOW

Begin to acknowledge the Word. Begin to speak the Word. Begin to acknowledge every good thing that is yours in Christ. That means walk around your house saying, "I am a new creature in Christ. Old things are passed away. Satan's dominion over my life has passed away. Sin's dominion over my life has passed away. The curse of poverty has passed away. The curse of Satan has passed away. The curse of sickness has passed away. I'm not under the curse. I have been redeemed. In Christ I have redemption. It is mine, and I have it now."

Blessed be the God and Father of our Lord Jesus Christ, who hath blessed us with all spiritual blessings in heavenly places in Christ.
Ephesians 1:3

...who has blessed us in Christ with every spiritual blessing that heaven itself enjoys.
Norlie

This is not something God is going to do or something that is going to happen when we get to heaven. It is something that is ours right now. All spiritual blessings belong to us right now.

In other words, you enjoy whatever heaven enjoys the moment you are in Christ. You are hooked up to heaven: the joy of heaven, the peace of heaven, the victory of heaven, and the glory of heaven. You are not of this world. You have been born of God! Hallelujah!

Where does all this happen? It doesn't happen in your body because you still have the same body. It doesn't happen in your head (in your mind) because you still have the same mind. It happens in your spirit, right down on the inside of you. That's the real you. The moment you are born again, your spirit is joined to Christ. Everything the Word says about anyone in Christ is true about you.

COMPLETE IN CHRIST

For in him dwelleth all the fullness of the Godhead bodily. And ye are complete in him, which is the head of all principality and power.
Colossians 2:9,10

So you have everything when you have Christ, and you are filled with God through your union with Christ....
Living Bible

The fullness of God is in Christ. The riches of God's glory and His treasury are in Him. The moment you are in Him, you have access to the fullness of God and you are complete in Him.

When you receive Jesus you have everything you need for the rest of your life. You are set for the rest of your life the moment you surrender to Jesus. He gives you wisdom, righteousness, sanctification, redemption — everything you need! You may be thinking, "But I don't look like that." Begin to acknowledge every good thing that is yours in Christ Jesus.

RIGHTEOUSNESS OF GOD IN CHRIST

For he hath made him to be sin for us, who knew no sin; that we might be made the righteousness of God in him.

2 Corinthians 5:21

In most churches you wouldn't have any trouble telling people, "Jesus died on the cross for you." But they doubt the second half of that verse: "...that we might be made the righteousness of God in him." If you believe the first half of the verse, why don't you believe the second half?

There is a reason Jesus was made to be sin for you. Paul is talking about your righteousness in Christ. Being righteous means that you are accepted by God, have right standing with

God, and are pleasing to Him. This gives you confidence in prayer and in facing the adversary, the accuser of the brethren. Paul is talking about acknowledging every good thing that is yours in Christ. These in Christ promises mean you have a choice whether you are going to follow the flesh or the Spirit.

> *There is therefore now no condemnation to those who are in Christ Jesus, who walk not after the flesh, but after the Spirit.*
>
> *Romans 8:1*

> *For the law of the Spirit of life in Christ Jesus hath made me free from the law of sin and death.*
>
> *Romans 8:2*

> *Who hath delivered us from the power of darkness, and hath translated us into the kingdom of his dear Son: In whom we have redemption through his blood, even the forgiveness of sins.*
>
> *Colossians 1:13,14*

Paul is talking about something that has already been done. Our faith becomes effective as we acknowledge every good thing that is in us in Christ Jesus.

A SPIRITUAL DEPOSIT — NOW

If you are still believing and confessing, "I know Jesus is wonderful, but I am just a lowly little worm and I can't do anything," you have missed the whole point. Paul is trying to tell you to acknowledge every good thing that is in you in Christ. He is not talking about every good thing that is in Christ in heaven — He is talking about in you right now.

Jesus is no worm. If you are in Him, you cannot be a saved worm! The Bible says you are an heir of God and a joint-heir with Jesus Christ. When you are born again, a spiritual deposit is made in you. We have talked about some of this deposit: wisdom, righteousness, sanctification, redemption. The Apostle Paul begins all his letters by stating what God has done for you in Christ. After he declares what God has done for you in Christ, he declares who you are in Christ and what to do about it.

TRIUMPH ALWAYS

Now thanks be unto God, which always causeth us to triumph in Christ....

2 Corinthians 2:14

God's plan for you is to triumph always. Paul didn't say you would never have any tough times. I like what someone said years ago, "Tough times never last, but tough people do." Hallelujah! So how do you get to be tough?

> ***...Be strong in the Lord and in the power of his might.***
>
> *Ephesians 6:10*

You become strong by acknowledging who you are and what you have in Christ.

What do you need to do to always triumph in Christ? Acknowledge every good thing that is in you in Christ. When you get up in the morning, walk around your bedroom and say, "I give thanks unto the Father God right now that He always causes me to triumph in Christ. When the enemy comes against me one way, he must flee in seven ways."

God never said the enemy wouldn't try to come against you. Isaiah 54:17 says, "No weapon that is formed against thee shall prosper...." He didn't say you wouldn't have any weapons formed against you, but He said the weapons can't prosper! In other words, when adversity comes against you, you can declare, "No weapon formed against me shall prosper." Because your righteousness is of the Lord. The righteousness you have wasn't produced by you. It was produced by the Lord. God produced it for you in Christ.

RENEWING YOUR MIND

That ye put off concerning the former conversation [He's talking about your lifestyle.] the old man, which is corrupt according to the deceitful lusts.

Ephesians 4:22

Paul is saying, "Change the way you are living." You won't change the way you are living if you don't change the way you are talking. In other words, "Quit talking the way you used to talk."

Set a watch, O Lord, before my mouth...

Psalm 141:3

For by thy words thou shalt be justified, and by thy words thou shalt be condemned.

Matthew 12:37

Thou art snared with the words of thy mouth...

Proverbs 6:2

And be renewed in the spirit of your mind; And that ye put on the new man, which after God is created in righteousness and true holiness.

Ephesians 4:23,24

Paul is discussing who we are in Christ. He is saying, "Here is something you need to do. Put off the old nature, the old lifestyle." To put off is like taking off the old clothes. Then he says, "Put on the new man." He gives directions how to put on the new man, "And be renewed in the spirit of your mind."

The process of putting off the old and putting on the new takes place as you renew your mind and line your thinking up with the Word of God. We should always ask, "What does God's Word have to say about such-and-such? What does the Word say about me? What does the Word say that I have? Who does the Word say that I am? What do I need to do now?" We need to say what God says. We need to agree with God.

Second Corinthians 5:17 says you become a new creature in Christ, but Ephesians 4:24 says, "put on the new man." There is something we need to do to put on the new man. Why? Because the new man is who you are on the inside and who you are in Christ. Paul is saying, "Take what you are and what you have in Christ and put it on." How do you put on the new man? By renewing your mind with God's Word.

> You won't change the way you are living if you don't change the way you are talking.

Paul also says that the new man, "...is created in righteousness and true holiness," Ephesians 4:24. In other words, you are not trying to make the new man righteous and holy. He is saying, "The moment you are born again, you are a new creation, and you are created in righteousness and true holiness." Then he says, "put on the new man." Since you have been made a partaker of the divine nature, you are to put on the new man, who is created in righteousness and true holiness.

DETHRONE YOUR REASONING AND BODY

So what do you need to do? You don't need to make the new man righteous, but you need to put him on. How do you do that?

> *That the communication of thy faith may become effectual by the acknowledging of every good thing which is in you in Christ Jesus.*
>
> **Philemon 6**

What would happen if you made a list and started acknowledging every good thing that is yours in Christ? God already deposited every good thing in you when you were born again, but it is up to you to acknowledge what you have in Christ.

You must acknowledge who you are and what you have in Christ. Just because you are a believer doesn't mean you won't have any trouble with your flesh or your mind. Even as a born again, Spirit-filled believer, you still have to do something with your body. What did Paul say he did with his body?

> ***...I keep under my body, and bring it into***
> ***subjection...***
>
> > *1 Corinthians 9:27*

God is not going to do anything about your body or your mind. He already did the biggest work in your spirit (your inward man) when you were born again. God gave you His Word, which is full of life and power, and the Holy Ghost lives on the inside of you. You can do something with your body. Begin by acknowledging who you are in Christ and let the Holy Ghost rise up on the inside of you. When you agree with God, your inner man (your spirit) will rise up and dethrone the dominance of your body and your reasoning.

THE ENGRAFTED WORD

> ***Wherefore lay apart all filthiness and***
> ***superfluity of naughtiness, and receive with***
> ***meekness the engrafted word, which is able to***
> ***save your souls.***
>
> > ***James 1:21***

In James 1:21, Paul was speaking to believers. This must mean that after you are born again, your soul still isn't saved. People say, "We had so many souls saved." Not necessarily. People came forward. They might have received

Christ and been born again, but their soul wasn't saved. Even after you are born again, you still have to get your soul saved. Your soul is made up of your mind, will, and emotions.

James says to receive the Word with meekness. Meekness means to receive it with humility. In other words, humble yourself and be teachable. The engrafted Word has the ability to save, deliver, restore, and make your soul (your mind, will, and emotions) whole.

Why does James call the Word *the engrafted Word*? The Word doesn't work unless it is implanted. It won't work for you unless it is implanted on the inside of you. How do you get it implanted? By acknowledging every good thing that is in you in Christ. In other words, you stick with it and keep feeding and meditating on the Word.

> The Word doesn't work unless it is implanted.

FAITH IS AN ACT

But be ye doers of the word, and not hearers only, deceiving your own selves.

James 1:22

What does it mean to be a doer of the Word? When you see something in the Word, you just act on it. You start acting like the Word is true. You become a doer of that Word. Faith without works [or corresponding action] is dead (James 2:26). If the Word says something belongs to you, you can say, "I am going to act on it. I am going to act like it is so. It may not feel like it or look like it, but I am acting on it right now." As you acknowledge the Word, start acting like it is true. Smith Wigglesworth said, "Faith is an act."

> *For if any be a hearer of the word, and not a doer, he is like unto a man beholding his natural face in a glass [or in a mirror]: For he beholdeth himself, and goeth his way, and straightway forgetteth what manner of man he was.*
>
> *James 1:23,24*

What do you look at when you look in the mirror? You look at yourself. James is saying, "If you hear the Word, but you don't do it, it is like looking in the mirror, going your way and forgetting what you look like."

> *But whoso looketh into the perfect law of liberty, and continueth therein, he being not a forgetful hearer, but a doer of the word, this man shall be blessed in his deed.*
>
> *James 1:25*

SEE YOURSELF IN CHRIST

How do you become a doer of the Word? You look into the mirror of the Word, which James calls "the perfect law of liberty." When you get up in the morning, look up about ten in Christ scriptures, look in the mirror, and acknowledge them. Look in the mirror — the perfect law of liberty. When you look into the mirror of the Word, it will make you free. One translation says, "Look and keep on looking."

When you keep on looking, there is a reflection and you see yourself in Christ. You see what God has done for you in Christ and suddenly, you see yourself free. You won't possess any more than you can see. If you continue to see yourself as a failure, unrighteous, unworthy, defeated, and confused, you will continue to live it out.

> If you keep looking into the Word, it will save, deliver, heal, and restore your soul.

God can tell you over and over what He has done for you in Christ and who you are in Christ.

As long as you continue to see yourself as a failure, unrighteous, unworthy, defeated, sick, or poor, you will stay in that condition. While you go by your thinking and feelings, God is saying, "Acknowledge every good thing that is in you in Christ. Renew your mind and put on the new man created in righteousness, victory, blessing, and holiness." When you get up in the morning, look in the Word. When you have a lunch break, open your Bible. If you have a fifteen minute break, open your Bible. This is what it takes to be blessed.

EVERYTHING WE NEED

...his divine power hath given unto us all things that pertain unto life and godliness...

2 Peter 1:3

God has deposited everything in you, through His Word, that you will ever need for life and godliness. He didn't say you have been given all things that pertain to heaven. No, you have been given all things that pertain to life and godliness right now!

...through the knowledge of him that called us to glory and virtue: Whereby are given unto us exceeding great and precious promises: that by these ye might be partakers of the divine nature, having escaped the corruption that is in this world through lust.

2 Peter 1:4

Peter is saying, "God has given you everything you need for life and godliness in the Word." James said, "You need to take these exceeding great and precious promises and get them engrafted on the inside of you. These promises will save your soul."

> ***Thy word have I hid in mine heart, that I might
> not sin against thee.***
>
> ***Psalm 119:11***

In other words, the more of the Word you have in you, the less trouble you will have with sin. To give mental assent to the Word won't work. James said for the Word to work for you, you need to, "Lay aside all filthiness and superfluity of naughtiness," James 1:21. If you have 50 percent Word and 50 percent filthiness and superfluity of naughtiness, the Word won't work for you. It will have some effect, but you need to get 100 percent of the Word into you.

THE WORD WORKS

If you keep looking into the Word, it will save, deliver, heal, and restore your soul. It will bring the blessing of God. Acknowledge who you are and what you have in Christ.

> ***For the word of God is quick, and powerful, and
> sharper than any two-edged sword, piercing
> even to the dividing asunder of soul and spirit,
> and of the joints and marrow, and is a discerner
> of the thoughts and intents of the heart.***
>
> ***Hebrews 4:12***

Nothing can separate your soul and your spirit but the Word. You might ask, "Why do they need to be separated?" God says you are a new creature in Christ. He says you have been made righteous and triumphant, but your mind is in disagreement. Your circumstances are in disagreement. Your feelings are in disagreement, but the Word is like a sharp sword. It will cause your circumstances and feelings to agree with God.

> *Think not that I am come to send peace on earth: I came not to send peace, but a sword.*
>
> *Matthew 10:34*

The sword will reach into your soul and separate and cut things out that are hindering you from fulfilling the will of God and being blessed. Ephesians 6:17 talks about, "...the sword of the Spirit, which is the word of God." The Word will cut controlling influences off of your life and will cut things out of your soul that are not in agreement with God's Word.

> The sword of the Spirit cuts controlling influences from your life.

What happens when you begin to acknowledge, "I am who God says I am. God says that I am an overcomer, so I say I am an overcomer. God says I have been made righteous, so I say right now, I am the righteousness of God in Christ"? The sword of the Spirit cuts controlling influences from your life.

REASON TO SHOUT

God is not a man, that he should lie; neither the son of man, that he should repent: hath he said, and shall he not do it? Or hath he spoken, and shall he not make it good.

Numbers 23:19

There is no way God can lie. If you find out what the Word says and you receive the engrafted Word, God will perform it in your life.

Behold, I have received commandment to bless: and he hath blessed; and I cannot reverse it. He hath not beheld iniquity in Jacob, neither hath he seen perverseness in Israel: the Lord his God is with him, and the shout of a king is among them.

Numbers 23:20,21

Once you know your covenant and who you are in Christ, there will be the shout of a king! If the Israelites were shouting under the Old Covenant, you have even more to shout about in the New Covenant. Just as God looked at the Israelites in the Old Covenant, He looks at you in Christ. He sees you as the righteousness of Christ. Balaam got a glimpse of the people the way God saw them. He didn't see iniquity in them.

The communication of faith will become effectual as you acknowledge every good thing that is in you in Christ!

What does this mean to you? If you have been made the righteousness of God in Christ, God sees no iniquity in you. You have reason to shout! It's time to get the Bible out and say, "Devil, if you can't read, let me read to you!" The communication of faith will become effectual as you acknowledge every good thing that is in you in Christ! Hallelujah!

WHAT YOU HAVE NOW IN CHRIST

God is planting a whole new crop of righteousness, wisdom, redemption, sanctification, blessing, joy, and victory on the inside of you. Put on the new man by declaring who you are in Christ. Make this confession of faith and acknowledge some of the things you have now in Christ.

I am who God says I am. I have what God says I have. I acknowledge right now by faith every good thing that is mine in Christ. I am a new creation in Christ. Old things have passed away. A whole new world has opened up to me in Christ, in the Spirit. I have been born again. I have been born of God. Old habits, attitudes, and controlling influences are broken and cut away from my life by the sword of the Spirit, which is the Word of God.

I acknowledge every good thing that is mine in Christ right now. I have been made the righteousness of God in Christ. Victory is mine now in Christ. In Him I am more than a conqueror. I have been refathered. God is my Father. I am righteous. I am strong in the Lord and in the power of His might.

I have been redeemed from the curse of the law. Christ has redeemed me from all iniquity. The law of the Spirit of life in Christ has made me free from the law of sin and death. I am free. I am righteous. Right now I am victorious. I am in Christ, and Christ is in me. I am blessed with every spiritual blessing in Christ right now. I am the workmanship of God, created in Christ Jesus. I receive with meekness the engrafted Word which is saving my soul. I am a doer of the Word. I am who God says I am. I am complete in Christ. In Him I am strong. In Him I am free. In Him I am blessed!

There is not one thing in me
that the Blood doesn't cleanse.
- Smith Wigglesworth

Neither by the blood of goats and
calves, but by His own blood He
entered in once into the holy place,
having obtained eternal redemption
for us.
Hebrews 9:12, KJV

16

FAITH IN THE BLOOD OF JESUS

Whom God hath set forth to be a propitiation through faith in his blood, to declare his righteousness for the remission of sins that are past, through the forbearance of God; To declare, I say, at this time his righteousness: that he might be just, and the justifier of him which believeth in Jesus...by the law of faith.

Romans 3:25-27

What a wonderful sight it is to see a space shuttle launch. You can see it rise slowly, then rocket into another world. The power, the sound, and the sight are fascinating. The giant fuel cells that propel it are necessary to get it out of this atmosphere into outer space. The shuttle leaves the law of gravity behind and enters a world of weightlessness. I like to compare that to "faith in the blood of Jesus." Faith in His blood is the power and the vehicle that launches the believer into the very presence of

> Faith in His blood is the power and the vehicle that launches the believer into the very presence of God.

God. We are launched into another realm where the new law of faith rules. The law of sin and death is broken by the law of the Spirit of life in Christ Jesus. The weight of sin that once held you down is broken and you are free. Think of the possibilities and the power in the blood of Jesus.

> *Faith is largely dependent on knowledge. If knowledge of what the blood can accomplish is not accurate, then faith expects little, and the more powerful effects of the blood are limited.*
>
> *Andrew Murray*

As we study the Word of God our faith grows. When we see clearly what Jesus has done for us through His blood, we begin our ascent into the realm of God. The blood of Jesus carries everything He has done for us. The blood of Jesus has many different ingredients and applications, which are applied by faith. God is a faith God and faith is what pleases Him. Faith opens the door to the supernatural. Faith is built on accurate knowledge (Romans 10:17). There is no such thing as ignorant faith. There is no such thing as silent faith. Faith has a voice (Mark 11:23). We honor the blood of Jesus as we lift our voice in faith declaring what it has and what it is accomplishing. The spoken Word of God is the voice of the blood covenant. Every Word has blood in it. The blood must be applied by faith. According to your faith so be it to you. There is no such thing as passive faith. Faith is an act. Faith acts like the Bible is true. Live by faith and continually apply the blood. There is power in the blood. We act in faith like the blood of Jesus has purchased our redemption.

"...The blood of Jesus Christ his Son cleanses us from all sin," 1 John 1:7. The blood in your body circulates from head to toe every 23 seconds. The blood carries life itself. It carries in the nutrients you need to live and it also carries out the garbage. The blood of Jesus circulates throughout the Body of Christ. We need one another. We need to be assembled together and we need to fellowship with other believers (Hebrews 10:25). There is some assembly required. I feel sorry for people who think they can make it on their own. We need other strong believers to fellowship with around the Word of God. Then the blood of Jesus circulates and takes care of life and health for us.

INGREDIENTS IN THE BLOOD

When we look at the New Testament, we see a full print out of the ingredients that are in the blood of Jesus. We can see what God sees in the blood. In order to purchase a million dollar life insurance policy, they would require a sample of your blood before you would be approved for the policy. They would send the blood to the lab to study it. Under powerful microscopes they would see what ingredients are in your blood. A few days later you would receive a full-page print out with a detailed description of what is in your blood.

> You will be launched into a new level of victory and blessing as you apply the blood.

A thorough investigation of the blood of Jesus reveals every necessary ingredient for full salvation. There is righteousness, forgiveness, redemption, sanctification, healing, victory, blessing, boldness, prosperity, and power in the blood of Jesus!

...by the blood (that sealed, ratified) the everlasting agreement (covenant, testament). Strengthen (complete, perfect) and make you what you ought to be and equip you with

everything good that you may carry out His will...

> *Hebrews 13:20-21, Amplified*

Through the blood of the everlasting covenant you will be made perfect in every good work to do His will. You will be launched into a new level of victory and blessing as you apply the blood constantly with boldness and full assurance of faith (Hebrews 10:19-25)!

And the veil in the temple was rent in twain from the top to the bottom.

> *Mark 15:38*

Having therefore brethren, boldness to enter into the holiest by the blood of Jesus, By a new and living way, which he hath consecrated for us, through the veil, that is to say, his flesh;

> *Hebrews 10:19-20*

IN CHRIST – ACCESS TO THE FATHER

When Jesus was crucified the veil in the temple that separated man from the Holy of Holies was torn from the top to the bottom. This signified that the Holy place was open for every man to enter into the closest fellowship with God. In Hebrews, the Apostle Paul says that veil was the body of Jesus. When His body was broken for us, we were granted access into Christ. When His blood was shed, we were accepted in Christ. In Him we have the closest fellowship with the Father God. God sees us through the blood of Jesus and welcomes us in His presence. The veil in the temple was the body of Jesus and we are in Christ. When He was wounded we were engrafted into Him. Now we are new creatures in Christ. We are the righteousness of God in Christ.

THE BLOOD OF HIS CROSS

It was through what his Son did that God cleared a path for everything to come to him-all things in heaven and on earth-for Christ's death on the cross has made peace with God for all by His blood. This includes you who were once so far away from God. You were his enemies and hated him and were separated from him by your own evil thoughts and actions, yet now he has brought you back as his friends. He has done this through the death on the cross of his own human body, and now as a result Christ has brought you into the very presence of God, and you are standing there

before Him with nothing left against you-
nothing left that he could even chide you for.
Colossians 1:20-22 Living Bible

HONOR THE BLOOD OF JESUS

The King James Version says it this way in Colossians 1:20-22, "Through the blood of his cross…you are reconciled to God by Him…In the body of his flesh through death, to present you holy and unblameable and unreproveable in His sight." We as believers are accepted in the presence of God having perfect fellowship with the Father God because of what Christ has done for us. God sees us in Christ. In Him we have redemption through His blood (Colossians 1:14). Now we have full assurance of faith to go right into the very presence of God because we have been washed in the blood of Jesus. Ephesians 3:12, says, "In whom we have boldness and access with confidence by the faith of him. By faith in the blood of Jesus we are in Christ. Let us honor the blood of Jesus and confess daily who we are and what we have in Christ Jesus.

IN CHRIST SCRIPTURES
Who You Are and What You Have In Christ

IN CHRIST

Romans 3:24	Gal. 2:4	1 Thess. 4:16
Romans 8:1	Gal. 3:26	1 Thess. 5:18
Romans 8:2	Gal. 3:28	1 Tim. 1:14
Romans 12:5	Gal. 6:15	2 Tim. 1:9
1 Cor. 1:2	Eph. 1:3	2 Tim. 1:13
1 Cor. 1:30	Eph. 1:10	2 Tim. 2:1
1 Cor 15:22	Eph. 2:6	2 Tim. 2:10
2 Cor. 1:21	Eph. 2:10	2 Tim. 3:15
2 Cor. 2:14	Eph. 2:13	Phile. 1:6
2 Cor. 3:14	Eph. 3:6	1 Peter 1:8
2 Cor. 5:17	Phil. 3:13, 14	
2 Cor. 5:19	Col. 1:28	

IN HIM

Acts 17:28	Col. 2:6	1 John 3:3
John 1:4	Col. 2:7	1 John 3:5
John 3:15,16	Col. 2:9,10	1 John 3:6
2 Cor. 1:20	1 John 2:5	1 John 3:24
2 Cor. 5:21	1 John 2:6	1 John 4:13
Eph. 1:4	1 John 2:8	1 John 5:14, 15
Eph. 1:10	1 John 2:27	1 John 5:20
Phil. 3:9	1 John 2:28	

REFERENCES

Adams, Jay E. *The New Testament in Everyday English.* Baker Book House, Grand Rapids, Michigan, 1979.

Amplified Bible. Zondervan Publishing House, Grand Rapids, Michigan, 1972.

American Standard Bible. Thomas Nelson and Sons, New York, New York, 1901.

Barclay, William. New Testament Words. Westminster Press. Philadelphia, Pennsylvania, 1974.

Barclay, William. *The New Testament A New Translation.* Collins, London, England, 1968.

Barth, Markus. *Anchor Bible.* Double Day and Company, Inc., Garden City, New York, 1974.

Beck, William. *The Holy Bible In The Language of Today.* A.J. Holman Company, New York, New York, 1976.

Blackwelder, Boyce. *Letters From Paul An Exegetical Translation.* Warner Press, London, England, 1944.

Cressman, A. *Good News for the World.* SOON! Publications, Bombay, India, 1969.

Deane, Anthony C. *St. Paul and His Letters.* Hodder and Stoughton, London, England, n.d.

Goodspeed, Edgar J. *The New Testament, An American Translation.* University of Chicago, Chicago, Illinois, 1923.

Gordon, A.J. *In Christ.* Wade Pickren Publications, Revised 1983.

Hayman, Henry. *Four Volume Series, Letters of Apostle Paul.* Spirit to Spirit Publications, Tulsa, Oklahoma, 1982.

Jordan, Clarence. *The Cotton Patch Version of Paul's Epistles.* Association Press, New York, New York, 1968.

Laubach, Frank C. *The Inspired Letters in Clearest English.* Thomas Nelson and Sons, New York, New York, 1956.

Minirth, Frank, Paul Meier, and Stephen Arterburn. *The Complete Life Encylopedia.* Thomas Nelson Publisher, Nashville , Tennessee , 1995.

Moffatt, James. *The Holy Bible Containing the Old and New Testaments.* Double Day and Company, Inc., Garden City, New York, 1926.

New American Standard Bible. A.J. Holman, New York, New York, 1971.

New English Bible. Oxford University Press, Oxford, England, 1961.

Noli, Fan. S. *The New Testament of Our Lord and Savior Jesus Christ.* Albanian Orthodox Church In America, Boston, Massachusetts, 1961.

Norlie, Olaf M. *Norlie's Simplified New Testament in Plain English - For Today's Readers.* Zondervan Publishing House, Grand Rapids Michigan, 1961

Phillips, J.B. *The New Testament in Modern English.* The Macmillan Company, New York, New York, 1958.

Revised Standard Bible. Thomas Nelson and Sons, New York, New York, 1953

Rotheram, J.B. *The Emphasized Bible.* Kregel Publications, Grand Rapids, Michigan, 1976.

Stalker, James. *The Life of ST. Paul.* Zondervan Corporation. Grand Rapids, Michigan, 1983.

Stewart, James. *A Man in Christ.* Baker Book House. Grand Rapids Michigan, 1975.

Taylor, Ken. *The Living Bible.* Tyndale House Publishers, Inc., Wheaton, Illinois, 1971.

The Distilled Bible/New Testament. Paul Benjamin Publishing Company, Stone Mountain, Georgia, 1980.

The Holy Bible, New International Version. Zondervan Publishing House, Grand Rapids, Michigan, 1978.

The Jerusalem Bible. Double Day and Company, Inc., Garden City, New York, 1968.

The New Testament English Version for the Deaf. Baker Book House, Grand Rapids, Michigan, 1978.

The Translator's New Testament. The British and Foreign Bible Society, London, England, 1977.

The Twentieth Century New Testament. Revised Edition. The Fleming H. Revell Company, New York, New York, 1909.

Verkuyl, Gerrit. *The Holy Bible, The New Berkely Version, Revised Edition in Modern English.* Zondervan Publishing House, Grand Rapids, Michigan, 1969.

Vine's Complete Expository Dictionary of Old and New Testament Words. Thomas Nelson, Inc., Nashville, Tennessee, 1984, 1996.

Way, Arthur S. *The Letters of St. Paul to the Seven Churches and Three Friends with the Letter to the Hebrews.* Sixth Edition. Macmillan and Company, New York, New York, 1926.

Weymouth, Richard Francis. *The New Testament.* James Clark and Company, London, England, 1909.

Williams, Charles G. *The New Testament.* Moody Press, Chicago, Illinois, 1978.

Williams, Charles Kingsley. *The New Testament, A New Translation in Plain English.* Longmans, Green, and Co., London, England, 1952.

Purchasing and Contact Information

MARK HANKINS MINISTRIES
P.O. BOX 12863
ALEXANDRIA, LA 71315

Phone: 318.448.4500
Fax: 318.443.2948

Email: contact@markhankins.org

Visit us on the web:
www.markhankins.org

Mark Hankins Ministries Publications

SPIRIT-FILLED SCRIPTURE STUDY GUIDE
A comprehensive study of scriptures in over 120 different translations on topics such as: Redemption, Faith, Finances, Prayer and many more!

THE POWER OF IDENTIFICATION WITH CHRIST
This book focuses on the reality of redemption and your new identity in Christ. As a new creature, you have everything you need inside of you to succeed in life!

THE SPIRIT OF FAITH
If you only knew what was on the other side of your mountain, you would move it! Having a spirit of faith is necessary to do the will of God and fulfill your destiny.

NEVER RUN AT YOUR GIANT
WITH YOUR MOUTH SHUT
When David ran at Goliath, there was a war of words going on. In this book, we learn that winning the war of words is necessary to winning the fight of faith.

11:23 - THE LANGUAGE OF FAITH
Never underestimate the power of one voice! Over 100 inspirational, mountain-moving quotes to "stir up" the spirit of faith in you.

TAKING YOUR PLACE IN CHRIST
Many Christians talk about what they are trying to be and what they are going to be. This book is about who you are NOW as a believer in Christ.

**ACKNOWLEDGING EVERY GOOD THING
THAT IS IN YOU IN CHRIST**
This mini-book encourages every believer to have a daily confession or acknowledgment of who they are in Christ.

REVOLUTIONARY REVELATION
This book provides excellent insight on how the spirit of wisdom and revelation is mandatory for believers to access their call, inheritance, and authority in Christ.

LET THE GOOD TIMES ROLL
This Book focuses on the five key factors to heaven on earth: The Holy Spirit, Glory, Faith, Joy, and Redemption. The Holy Spirit is a genius. If you will listen to Him, He will make you look smart.

About the Author

Mark and Trina Hankins travel nationally and internationally preaching the Word of God with the power of the Holy Spirit. Their message centers on the spirit of faith, who the believer is in Christ, and the work of the Holy Spirit.

Mark Hankins' daily radio program, "Taking Your Place in Christ," is heard across the United States. It is also made available internationally, via the internet at www.markhankins.org.

Trina is an anointed praise and worship leader and recording artist. She has recorded two albums: *A Place by the Father and Be It unto Me.*

Mark and Trina have also pastored for 23 years, but now they are traveling extensively around the United States and Internationally full-time. Their son, Aaron Hankins and his wife, Errin Cody, are now the pastors of Christian Worship Center in Alexandria, Louisiana. Their daughter Alicia Moran and her husband, Caleb, serve as directors of Mark Hankins Ministries.

Acknowledgements

Special Thanks To

My wife, Trina

My son, Pastor Aaron Hankins and his wife,
Errin Cody

their daughters, Avery Jane and Macy Claire

My daughter, Alicia Moran and her husband, Caleb

their son, Jaiden Mark

My dad, Pastor B.B. Hankins, who is now in heaven
with the Lord

My mom, Velma Hankins

My wife's parents, Pastor William and Ginger
Behrman